THE BEAST WITHIN

The
BEAST

Neil Boyd

WITHIN

WHY MEN ARE VIOLENT

GREYSTONE BOOKS

Douglas & McIntyre Publishing Group

Vancouver/Toronto/New York

Greystone Books
A division of Douglas & McIntyre Ltd.
2323 Quebec Street, Suite 201
Vancouver, British Columbia V5T 4S7

Canadian Cataloguing in Publication Data
Boyd, Neil, 1951–
The beast within
Includes bibliographical references and index.
ISBN 1–55054–766–6
1. Men—Psychology. 2. Masculinity. 3. Violence. I. Title.
BF692.5.B69 2000   155.6′32   C00–910149–7
Library of Congress Cataloguing-in-Publication information is available.

Editing by Nancy Flight
Jacket and text design by Peter Cocking
Jacket photograph by Chick Rice
Printed and bound in Canada by Friesens
Printed on acid-free paper ∞

The following sources have given permission for quoted material: From "Natural History" by Audrey Thomas in *Real Mothers*, published by Talon Books. Copyright © 1981. Reprinted by permission of the author. From *The Beak of the Finch: A Story of Evolution in Our Time* by Jonathan Weiner. Copyright © 1995. Reprinted by permission of Alfred A. Knopf, a Division of Random House, Inc. From *Demonic Males: Apes and the Origins of Human Violence*. Copyright © 1996 by Richard Wrangham and Dale Peterson. Reprinted by permission of Houghton Mifflin Company. All rights reserved. From *Larry's Party* by Carol Shields. Copyright © 1997. Reprinted by permission of Random House of Canada Limited.

Every attempt has been made to trace accurate ownership of copyrighted material in this book. Errors and omissions will be corrected in subsequent editions, provided that notification is sent to the publisher.

The publisher gratefully acknowledges the support of the Canada Council and of the British Columbia Ministry of Tourism, Small Business and Culture. The publisher also wishes to acknowledge the financial support of the Government of Canada through the Book Publishing Industry Development Program (BPIDP) for its publishing activities.

Contents

For my father, Bill Boyd, and my father-in-law, Ted Hocking

Acknowledgements

There are many people to thank for their contributions to this book. Kim McArthur and Charis Wahl provided early support and much useful criticism of this project. Dean Cooke has been consistently encouraging and helpful during the five years that this book has been a work in progress. Rob Sanders and Nancy Flight at Greystone Books have been similarly encouraging and constructive in their analyses of the work.

There are many people with whom I have spoken and corresponded in relation to the ideas expressed in the following pages; these men and women may not agree with all or even much of what I am arguing here, but their insights, and in some cases their written work, have helped me a great deal: Robert Pool, John Archer, Dave Albert, Doug Coleman, Debbie Brill, Gordon Cross, Martin Daly, and Margo Wilson. I'd also like to thank a few of my colleagues at Simon Fraser University: Barry Beyerstein, Margaret Jackson, Paul Brantingham, Gail Anderson, Kim Rossmo, Liz Elliott, and Simon Verdun-Jones.

My extended family has been particularly helpful in providing me (advertently and inadvertently) with a constant source of information about the complex interactions of biology and environment: Bill and Rose; Betty, Ted, and Stella; Ian, Bruce, and Tom; Elsie, Virginia, Warren, and Mary; John, Nia, Colin, and Barbara; Jacob and Kieran; Margaret, Chris, Marianne, Jeremy, and Madeleine; Kirstin and Paul; Sara, Scott, Dave, and Heather; Morgan and Simon; Carla, Bev, Darlene, Robbie, Fran, Layla, Tim, Rob, and Deb; Maddy and Elise; Cam and Katherine; John and Pat; and Dave and Chris.

Most important, I'd like to thank my wife, Isabel Otter, whose editorial work, insight, and love have been critical to the successful completion of this book.

Chapter One
The Trouble with Men

A few years ago, in the city, she had come home from
school and announced, at dinner, that a policeman had come
to the school and given a talk about "strangers."
Her mother and father glanced quickly at one another. A little girl,
her lunchbox beside her, had been found dead in a ditch.
"And what are strangers?" asked her father gently, curious as to
what she had been told, yet wanting to keep the story light.
The child's reply was very serious.
"Strangers are usually men."

AUDREY THOMAS, "NATURAL HISTORY"

Around 6:30 A.M. on October 8, 1997, in a suburb of Vancouver, British Columbia, Doug Holtam got out of bed, got dressed, and went out to the porch to get a hammer. He then went back into his bedroom and bashed his sleeping wife, Leonora, in the head. She was pregnant with their third child.

Her moaning awakened their 6-year-old daughter, Jenny. When she walked into her parents' bedroom to see what was going on,

I

Holtam turned his weapon on his daughter and hit her several times in the head. There was blood everywhere. With two members of his family dead or dying, Holtam went to find his 8-year-old son, Cody. The boy was standing at the top of the stairs, outside his room. Holtam bludgeoned him with the hammer too and left him for dead, but he survived the attack.

After the killings, Holtam washed the blood off his hands and went to work. From the time the bodies were discovered, police suspected that Holtam was responsible. They arrested him on the day of the crime, but he was released for lack of evidence.

On the day of the funerals for his wife and daughter, Holtam explained to his grieving family that he needed to be alone. He then took the ferry to Victoria, on Vancouver Island, and joined his new lover, Shannon Goddard, designer of a western clothing line called Ride Hard Western Wear. That evening undercover police observed Holtam and Goddard slow dancing and kissing each other on the dance floor of a country and western bar.

Ms. Goddard stood by her man after hearing of his initial arrest and release. She sent him a hand-drawn heart with an arrow through it; in the centre of the heart were the words "I love you." Goddard also enclosed a note on Stay'n Save motel stationery saying, "I'll wait forever for you and love you longer. I love you so much, life will begin again when your [sic] with me."

Shannon Goddard will wait for a very long time. After an elaborate five-month sting investigation, in which police posed as members of an organized-crime ring, they tricked Holtam into a confession of his crime, which was secretly videotaped. As a result of this confession and DNA evidence linking the blood of his victims to his clothing, Holtam was convicted of first-degree murder in the fall of 1999 and sentenced to life imprisonment.

On the videotape Holtam explained that the day of the killings was just like any other normal day at work; he had coffee with a co-worker and didn't think too much about what he had done. He had no trouble sleeping that night or any subsequent night. His motive for the killings? "This is the honest truth—boredom," he said. He had fallen in love with another woman and he was bored with his married life.

This kind of violence is fundamentally male. A similar kind of violence by women is virtually unimaginable. Women never track down their entire families and kill them. As evolutionary psychologists Martin Daly and Margo Wilson explain, marital violence by men is very different from marital violence by women:

> Men often hunt down and kill spouses who have left them; women hardly ever behave similarly. Men kill wives as part of planned murder-suicides; analogous acts by women are almost unheard of. Men kill in response to revelations of wifely infidelity; women almost never respond similarly, although their mates are often more adulterous. Men often kill wives after subjecting them to lengthy periods of coercive abuse and assaults; the roles in such cases are seldom if ever reversed. Men perpetrate familicidal massacres, killing spouse and children together; women do not. . . . Unlike men, women kill male partners after years of suffering physical violence, after they have exhausted all available sources of assistance, when they feel trapped, and because they fear for their own lives.

Like so many instances of male violence, Holtam's murderous act was related to his sexuality, and sex is often at the root of male violence. Criminal records are filled with case after case of predatory men, acting violently for reasons connected to their sexuality. The following narrative is another example of this typically male kind of violence.

On October 4, 1960, Kay Chouinor, a 26-year-old housekeeper in the small mining town of Timmins, Ontario, went for a ride with Mickey Feener, an unemployed labourer, in what he said was his new red sports car. Mickey soon confided in Miss Chouinor that he had killed a girl in New Brunswick in late September; he had left her body in a ditch and driven off in her red sports car. When Kay Chouinor urged Mickey to turn himself in to the police, he hit her three times on the head with his metal flashlight and she passed out.

When Kay Chouinor regained consciousness, Mickey Feener struck her on the back of the neck several times with his hunting knife. He then plunged the knife through her throat; yet she remained alive. With his victim slumped dying in the front seat, Feener drove the stolen sports car some 30 kilometres outside of Timmins. He finally threw her body against some rocks to make sure that she was dead, breaking her hip in the process.

Mickey Feener was arrested in Timmins a few days later; he confessed immediately to killing Kay Chouinor. Police in New Brunswick informed Timmins police that Feener's earlier victim was missing her underpants, though like Kay Chouinor, she had not been sexually assaulted.

As it turned out, Mickey had been sent to jail for stealing several times during the 1950s. He had also been married between

1957 and 1959; his wife reported that he had a violent temper and that during one of their many quarrels he had grabbed her by the throat and almost strangled her.

Shortly after his arrest Feener shook his fist at an angry crowd of a thousand residents gathered outside the jail. In court he dressed in cowboy boots, his striped shirt open almost to his waist, a gold cross hanging from a chain around his neck. He laughed softly at times; during police evidence he covered his head with his one unshackled hand.

One psychiatrist said of Feener, "His long history of abnormal behavior from the time he was a boy and the type of behavior that this is . . . would suggest that the patient is a psychopathic personality." Another psychiatrist wrote of "his extremely poor judgement and control over his impulses which in turn are secondary to his structural brain pathology."

Mickey Feener was convicted of murder, after jury deliberations lasting fifteen minutes, and sentenced to death by hanging. He was hanged shortly after midnight on June 13, 1961, confessing to the murder of a third young woman just hours before he died. He had taped photos of eight young women on the dashboard of the stolen red sports car, and only three of them were the victims he had confessed to killing. Police were never able to locate the other five but suspected that Feener was responsible for more than the three killings he had confessed to.

Mickey Feener was like most human beings who are violent; he was male, he wasn't especially capable, he had poor social skills, and his childhood was characterized by abuse and neglect. Both his parents deserted him and he was institutionalized at an early age. When he was 12 years old he was examined by a psychiatrist for the province to determine whether he should be placed in a training school for neglected, dependent, and delinquent children. Dr. E. P. Brison determined that Mickey Feener's IQ was 64; he also noted that young Mickey was "rather sly" and that he "ill-uses his younger brother when no one is looking." Both in the regular school system and in training school, Mickey was repeatedly victimized by other children.

When he was 16 years old, Mickey Feener was released from training school and went to work on the farm of Russell Haines. Mr. Haines later said of Mickey, "While he was here I found him on the lazy side. . . . To see the boy he seemed to be normal, but when you talked to him and got to know him you could tell he wasn't quite normal. He had a vicious streak in him and he seemed to want to do damage. I used to send him to feed the horses and once I found one of the horses injured from a pitch fork. He left scratches on the horses' flanks that bled quite a bit." His grandmother was more direct in her assessment of Mickey when she wrote to the government to try to save his life: "I have known him from his childhood and it was noticeable from four years of age that he was a mental case."

On the environmental side, Mickey Feener was an abused and neglected child, shunted from one family to another. On the biological side, he had a low IQ and a lifelong history of troubled behaviour.

Once again, Mickey Feener's behaviour is inherently male; it would be inconceivable in a woman. Feener killed three women, not because they were abusing him or because they had wronged him in any way. In at least one case Feener removed his victim's underpants, either because he wanted them as a trophy or because of sexual curiosity. In those few circumstances in which women kill, they never engage in such behaviour; women do not kill sequentially and take their victims' underwear.

Environment versus Biology

Unfortunately, most researchers, policymakers, and practitioners do not look at all the relevant factors in the very serious social problem of male violence. Our society has rejected a middle ground, in which both environment and biology are seen as integrally linked to male violence, preferring a polarized position in which either environment or biology—usually environment—is seen as the critical factor.

These polarized positions have led to the belief that if a man or woman is violent, it must be because of a wretched environment or a psychological disorder. Perhaps we want simple answers; we want to believe in a simple cause-and-effect relationship when the reality is muddier. When violence occurs we want to be able to point to an obvious cause: an abusive parent, an abusive partner, a psychopathic personality. There is a kind of comfort in this talk; we can distinguish between victims and offenders, simultaneously satisfying our desires for explanation and for moral denunciation of violent behaviour.

As a result, we now have "syndromes" to explain behaviour. There is a plethora of these syndromes or disorders for both male and female violence: battered women's syndrome, attention deficit disorder, psychopathic personality disorder, multiple personality disorder, drug abuse, the existence of the xyy chromosome, post-traumatic stress disorder, premenstrual stress, repressed memory, and Stockholm syndrome. Some of these syndromes and disorders simply capture the sordid or tragic circumstances of unhappy lives—for example, years of alcohol and drug abuse and repeated involvement in destructive relationships.

The difficulty with these explanations is, first, that they represent only one side of the coin, and second, that many are without systematic empirical support. It is in the realm of environment that the most bizarre and foolish explanations for human behaviour have arisen. Biologically driven explanations for antisocial behaviour—attention deficit disorder, psychopathic personality disorder, and the xyy chromosome theory—can be and have been tested for reliability and validity, thereby depending upon the tenets of science for their legitimacy. In contrast, environmental and cultural explanations—battered women's syndrome, multiple personality disorder, post-traumatic stress disorder, and repressed memory—haven't been tested. Consider, for example, the idea that memory can be repressed.

The Fraud of Repressed Memory

The theory of repressed memory holds that many people have trouble coping with everyday life for reasons that have not yet entered their consciousness. With the help of a therapist (who may or may not have professional training at an accredited college or university), these people gradually recover memories of early sexual abuse that is said to have coloured the individual's interactions with the social world from that point onward. With the intervention of the therapist, the victim works at uncovering the totality of the abuse (peeling away the layers of the onion) and then, to make herself (and occasionally himself) strong again, she confronts the source of all her inadequacies—usually a father, stepfather, uncle, or reasonable facsimile.

Unhappily, childhood sexual abuse is not uncommon. And there is credible evidence that human beings forget some past events. But science tells us that people are extremely unlikely to forget a very traumatic experience; science also tells us that forgotten incidents cannot be gradually recalled in stunning detail years afterward. Childhood experiences may or may not be forgotten, but they are rarely repressed. Repression itself—never mind the recovery of repression—is extremely unusual. Moreover, people have no capacity to recollect memories from three or four years of age or earlier.

But advocates of repressed memory would have us believe that they can recover long-forgotten trauma from the subconscious, where it has been festering and causing previously inexplicable behavioural problems. At the point of presumed recollection the trauma emerges in ever-expanding detail, demanding justice, typically in the form of criminal charges against the alleged aggressor, financial compensation, and more counselling (read economic and emotional dependence) for the victim.

Repressed memory didn't exist in the 1970s and was only coming into being in the late 1980s. It flourished in the early 1990s, spurred on by the 1988 book *The Courage to Heal,* a self-help prescriptive for incest survivors. The authors of that tome ask men and women how often they suffer from the following symptoms. You feel that you're bad, dirty, or ashamed? You feel powerless, like a victim? You feel that there's something wrong with you deep down inside; that if people really knew you, they would leave? You feel unable to protect yourself in dangerous situations? You have no sense of your own interests, talents, or goals? You have trouble feeling motivated? You feel you have to be perfect?

As social psychologist Carol Tavris has pointed out, lack of motivation and poor self-esteem may suggest a self-defeating personality disorder or someone who cares too deeply about others or simply an inability to function in present-day society. People with these characteristics are not very happy with themselves or their lives and can fairly be described as fragile and vulnerable. But the authors of *The Courage to Heal* go much further: they say that positive responses to these questions imply a history of incest.

Armed with a list of characteristics to look for in their patients, a phalanx of therapists has rushed to encourage supposed incest survivors and survivors of childhood sexual abuse to summon and exorcize the demons locked within—with the frequent consequence that a father, stepfather, or close relative is identified as an abuser, thus estranging patient from family members (who are said to be "in denial" if they raise doubts about the allegations). Even apparently qualified psychiatrists or psychologists engage in these practices—for example, Jungian dream therapists, unlocking the child from its cage—or worse.

A symbiotic relationship develops between the therapist and the patient. It takes time to uncover the memory (hence a steady source of income for the therapist). And not surprisingly, there is constant encouragement from the therapist to recover the memories and constant reassurance that what is wrong with one's life can be attributed to this early legacy of abuse. There is never any suggestion that personality characteristics might be genetic in origin; any weakness or limitation must be the consequence of another person's actions towards the "victim."

The notion of repressed memory has not withstood scientific scrutiny, and a strong opposition to it has emerged. The False Memory Syndrome Foundation has evidence of more than five hundred parents who share a common experience: only after being exposed to therapy did their children recall childhood sexual abuse. Most accusers are quite well educated and from middle-class families, fitting the profile of people who seek assistance from counsellors of one kind or another.

This excursion into repressed memory in Canada and the United States has caused a great deal of damage to families and has not helped at all in society's attempts to understand how and why male violence occurs; repressed memory is a sham that has taken us backwards. The criminal convictions that have been generated through claims of repressed memory are evidence of the continuing strength of a dangerous fallacy: the belief that environmental trauma necessarily causes inappropriate behaviour. Predictably, there is also no empirical evidence demonstrating that memory recovery therapy helps victims to improve their lives or to benefit in any way other than permitting them to talk endlessly about themselves and their problems. Moreover, some research suggests that such "therapeutic" interventions lead patients to become more disabled than they already are.

Stephen Mobley and His Ancestors

On February 17, 1991, Stephen Mobley walked into a Domino's Pizza Store in Oakwood, Georgia, with a gun. He cleaned out the cash register and then shot the store manager in the back of the neck. About a month later he confessed to police that he had committed the crime; he was charged with murder, punishable by death.

Stephen Mobley is the grandson of John and Cora Mae Mobley. John Mobley was a farmer and an alcoholic; he died from an illness that he contracted when he was drunk and overexposed to the cold. His wife, Cora Mae, was a strong-willed woman who lacked any value system. Cora Mae and John Mobley had three sons: Arthur, J. C., and Ralph. Once, with the assistance of J. C., Cora beat up Arthur's wife while her husband was away on a business trip. Cora also had many extramarital affairs and was very successful in business, becoming the owner of a coal company and a substantial amount of real estate.

Arthur was considered the most violent of the boys; he was an excessive drinker who was physically abusive in the extreme to his wife and children. He was also very successful in business, owning a racetrack, restaurants and lounges, and vending machines. J. C. too was an excessive drinker who had a volcanic temper. When he was young he served a short time in prison for a killing. It was also commonly taken for granted that he had caused his wife's death when he was about fifty.

Ralph, Stephen Mobley's father, was regarded as the most pleasant of the three boys. He was also, however, an excessive drinker who was physically and verbally abusive to his children, though only verbally abusive to his wife. Like his mother, Ralph had many extramarital affairs; he was a fairly successful business-man who apparently mellowed later in life but continued to have problems with alcohol.

Before committing the murder in Oakwood, Stephen Mobley had experienced a very troubled childhood and adolescence. He had been expelled from several public and private schools for in-appropriate behaviour. He spent ninety days in a mental hospital, and a therapeutic facility recommended that Stephen be made to live on his own. He then became involved in armed robbery, auto theft, and credit card forgery, committing at least six armed robberies before the Domino's Pizza killing. While in prison for the Domino's murder, he told a fellow inmate that he shot the em-ployee because he was crying and begging for his life. Young Mobley also had the word "Domino" tattooed on his back, hung a Domino's Pizza box top on the wall of his cell, and carried a domino in his pocket. He raped a fellow inmate twice and threatened a number of guards by telling them that they were beginning to look more and more like Domino's delivery boys.

Although the attorney for Stephen Mobley realized that his client's treatment throughout his childhood and adolescence must have had a detrimental effect, he decided to present evidence to suggest that his client's crime could be attributable to his genetic makeup. He was not arguing that this genetic history could be a defence but rather that it was a mitigating circumstance that would justify a life sentence rather than the death penalty. Specifically, counsel requested that preliminary neurological testing be per-formed to determine whether Mobley was suffering from an imbalance of any of a variety of neurochemicals—serotonin, adrenaline, noradrenalin, or monoamine oxidase A. There is some evidence that when borderline mental retardation is combined with imbalance in neurochemicals, unpredictable behaviour is the consequence, and counsel hoped to advance this theory on behalf of his client.

But tests showed that Mobley's IQ was 104, placing him well inside the normal range, and the judge hearing the case denied Mobley's attorney the right to call evidence in relation to such a theory. "The theory of genetic connection is not at a level of scientific acceptance that would justify its admission," the court concluded. Stephen Mobley remains on death row in Georgia.

With repressed memory, a theory of environmental trauma that has no scientific basis has been used under some circumstances to produce criminal convictions. But in the Mobley case, evidence of a genetic link was disallowed, even to mitigate the sentence.

Fordham University law professor Deborah Denno argues that there are a number of important reasons for the very different treatment of genetic evidence. First, to allow genetic evidence is to renew a historical association with Nazi abuses during the Holocaust. Second, to admit genetic evidence is to diminish the importance of free will in the commission of crime. Western systems of justice depend on the coincidence of *mens rea,* an evil intent or evil mind, with *actus reus,* an evil act, in order for there to be a valid criminal conviction. Third, if society allowed genetic evidence it would be, in some important sense, absolving the accused of the crime. "You are not responsible—your genes made you do it." Conversely, the court could take the position that this type of offender

should be penalized more than others because he is more dangerous and incorrigible than a more malleable person who has a less
threatening genetic background and who, accordingly, might be
susceptible to environmental influences.

The irony is that we believe environmental influences are more
important in shaping the violent conduct of the individual. But if
this is so, penalties for those whose conduct is environmentally
influenced ought to be increased to reflect the power of a bad upbringing. The lesson that we could learn from the use of evidence
of a genetic or environmental effect on violent behaviour would be
that more information is better than less. As long as the criminal
courts continue to allow evidence relating to an individual's environmental background, they should also allow the important di-
mension of genetic predisposition.

An important caveat: the admission of more information should
not be equated with excusing conduct or diminishing penalties.
Even if Stephen Mobley has a genetic predisposition to violence
that is substantially greater than that of most men, should society
downplay his guilt or lessen the penalty that would otherwise be
imposed? Similarly, even if a young man is abused or neglected and
then commits a crime as an adult, should his sentence be diminished or his conduct excused because of his unhappy past?

It is bad science and bad politics to allow such excuses. We
must try to understand the link between genes, environment, and
behaviour—that is the value of increasing the range of information
heard in criminal courts. It is greater understanding—not excusing
or diminishing violent conduct—that is to be gained from such an
exercise.

The Beast Within

Today the influence of biology is given little consideration in either the academic world or the agencies that deal directly with the effects of male violence. Those who study and write about violence or who counsel violent men rarely take the role of genetics into account. Sociologists, social workers, and criminologists develop their careers on the principle that violence has environmental roots. Anyone who draws attention to the relationship between biology and male violence is seen as a status quo apologist, wedded to the notion that male violence is a biologically determined inevitability.

In a previous book on murder and murderers I too dismissed the relevance of biology, confidently asserting that violence is simply a learned response and that "our culture has consistently rewarded men for aggression in a wide range of settings and circumstances."

The latter view is one to which I still subscribe, but in failing to consider the relevance of biology I was only looking at a part of the problem of male aggression, understanding what I wanted to understand, smugly wrapping myself in the view that only culture is a subject worthy of study. Martin Daly and Margo Wilson have pointed out the harms of such "biophobia," noting that the danger of such analysis resides in the essentially totalitarian suggestion that

> our social natures are pure cultural artifacts. We can therefore create any world we want, simply by changing "our socialization practices.". . . New, improved socialization practices will be designed by nice people with everyone's best interests at heart, and not by nasty self-interested despots.

This kind of social determinism also encourages a cult of victimization in which all of one's weaknesses and evils are ultimately traced to the actions of others. In this view, such flaws are the products of bad or inappropriate socialization, and the recognition of one's own inherent limitations is not encouraged or even seen as relevant.

As Robert Hughes has written in *Culture of Complaint*:

> To be vulnerable is to be invincible. Complaint gives you power—even when it's only the power of emotional bribery, of creating previously unnoticed levels of social guilt. . . . The range of victims available ten years ago—blacks, Chicanos, Indians, women, homosexuals—has now expanded to include every permutation . . . the blind, the lame and the short, or, to put it correctly, the differently abled, the other-visioned and the vertically challenged. Never before in human history were so many acronyms pursuing identity. It's as though all human encounter were one big sore spot, inflamed with opportunities to unwittingly give, and truculently receive, offence.

My own introduction to the importance of linking biology and behaviour began in an arena far removed from the realms of violence. When David Otter was about a year old he was diagnosed with spinal muscular atrophy. The physician who made the diagnosis told his parents that he would probably live only a year or two more.

Spinal muscular atrophy is classified as a disease of the lower and upper motor nerve cells that results in the wasting of muscle.

People who develop the disease in infancy often die during childhood, most frequently from respiratory complications.

The recessive gene that produces spinal muscular atrophy is carried by about 1 in every 85 human beings. If two carriers produce offspring, there is a 1 in 4 chance that their child will develop the disease. In other words, spinal muscular atrophy will appear in 1 of every 25,000 births.

I first met David Otter when he was 8 years old. He was flying a kite from his electric wheelchair, and I was struck by his vulnerability. When his chair went over bumpy ground, his head fell forward, the muscles in his neck unable to stop the momentum; he often needed help to right himself. I was also struck by his intelligence and humour; he was verbal, intense, and alert. But on that first meeting I could not have predicted the significant effect that he would have on the way I have come to look at the world.

The genetic heritage that gave David spinal muscular atrophy also provided him with his unusual abilities. His parents' attributes suggested that David would have more than his share of the mathematical and verbal abilities that we call intelligence. His father was the gold medalist in his graduating class at a prominent Canadian university; his mother graduated from one of the country's best law schools.

David's parents ensured that he was socially and intellectually involved in the community in every aspect of his life. There were wooden ramps to the front door of his home, an elevator, a van, and a series of customized wheelchairs. And David returned the caring and generosity with his determination and his cheerfulness.

In the end, however, the best environment could only postpone and minimize the effects of his disability; it could not overcome them. David died in 1983, from respiratory complications, at the age of 14. Both parts of the nature-nurture mix were clearly important, but who David was, and who all of us are, is more determined by our biology than many of our culture's experts have been willing to recognize.

The reluctance to consider biological explanations for human potential and behaviour is understandable, especially in the post–World War II era. Such explanations evoke the Nazi belief in genetic determinism and the notion that blacks are inferior to whites. Those who have argued for a biological basis for behaviour have, at least historically, argued for ideas that are intellectually absurd and morally repugnant.

Such viewpoints have yet to be extinguished from our culture. Racism, anti-Semitism, and "ethnic cleansing" are still with us. But denying the role of biology in male violence carries a different kind of danger. By diminishing the role of biology and overemphasizing the role of environment, our culture has abandoned the tenets of science in favour of the forces of political correctness. We have handed over our thinking about violence to ideologically driven theoreticians—those who believe in an environmentally influenced view of the world: men and women emerge from the womb with a genetic heritage but are best seen as vessels waiting to be formed by their experiences. The theoreticians of social science tell us that men are more violent than women only because they are encouraged to be aggressive, rewarded for their antisocial conduct in a wide range of settings and circumstances—from the football field to the corporate boardroom.

The late Marvin Wolfgang, probably the best-known and most frequently cited criminologist in the English-speaking world, argued that "neither biology or psychology can help to explain the overwhelming involvement in crime of men over women." The eminent anthropologist Marvin Harris wrote, in apparent defiance of what is known about male size, strength, and speed, "Knowing only the facts of human anatomy and biology, one could not predict that females would be the socially subordinate sex." Therapist Ron Thorne-Finch, in a chapter entitled "Why Are Men Violent?" in his book *Ending the Silence,* devoted three pages to biological and biosocial explanations of the phenomenon and a further fifty-seven pages to social and cultural explanations. These are only three of thousands of examples of social scientists who consistently reject any useful analytic role for biology in the production of male violence.

Their views are naive. In suggesting that the key to male violence is found in culture, these social scientists are indulging in the conceit that Darwin exposed a century ago, pompously declaring that we human beings have evolved beyond our mammalian ancestors. The point of this book is to suggest that the human male, like most other male apes, has a biological susceptibility to aggression and violence. It is a susceptibility, not biology as destiny—what Stephen Jay Gould has described in another context as "biological potentiality."

Biology plays a critical role in male violence. First, male violence has been present throughout history, beginning with our ape ancestors. There are strong similarities between the aggression of male apes and the aggression of male human beings. The practice of "ethnic cleansing" is virtually identical to chimpanzee raids on neighbouring clans of chimps. We are not very different, emotionally or intellectually, from our closest relatives, the chimpanzees. Moreover, recent DNA evidence indicates that we are genetically more similar to chimpanzees than chimpanzees are to orangutans or gorillas.

Male violence has been a hallmark of all human cultures. At the dawn of the third millennium, in every country in the world, men are overwhelmingly responsible for violent crime. And it has always been this way—in 1st-century Rome, in 13th-century England, in Idi Amin's Uganda, and in contemporary Scandinavia. Think of the most horrific crimes from our recent past: an epidemic of rape in South Africa; three Texas racists tying a black man to their car and dragging him to his death; the brutal murder of Mathew Shepard in the western United States, killed simply because he was gay; in Canada, Paul Bernardo's kidnapping, rape, and murder of teenage girls. And then there are the mass murders and acts of terrorism: Oklahoma City and the killing of 168 men, women, and children in the demented hope that a second American revolution would be launched; genocides in Rwanda, Indonesia, and Kampuchea; the Pan Am bombing over Lockerbie, Scotland; the Air India bombing over the North Atlantic.

The "age of the goddess" in Minoan Crete and Margaret Mead's Samoa have been offered as two cultures in which male violence was virtually nonexistent. But accounts of Minoan Crete, which do point to a remarkably civilized society that was less violent than most, still mention human sacrifice, cannibalism, and the burning to the ground of most major settlements, and Margaret Mead's idyllic vision of Samoa has been contradicted by more recent research.

Throughout history, the perpetrators of the most vile and savage crimes always have been and still are almost exclusively male. In fact, if men were not included in criminal justice statistics, crime would hardly be an object of social concern and the percentage of the global population in jail would be less than one-tenth of what it is today. Even in countries with low rates of violent crime—Britain, Denmark, and Japan—men remain responsible for about 90 per cent of the loss of life that does occur.

Moreover, throughout history, the quality and character of male violence has differed from the quality and character of female violence. Women tend to kill their partners after a legacy of abuse or after abusing alcohol and other drugs. Men hunt down and kill their partners; women almost never engage in such behaviour. Men kill after revelations of adultery; women do not. Men kill their partners after consistently subjecting them to abuse; women do not. Men perpetrate familicidal massacres, killing spouse and children; women do not. Men kill strangers; women do not. Men kill during sexual assaults; women do not.

The second biological factor in male violence is related to sex differences. Boys and girls play in very different ways, as do adult men and women. Careful research studies, conducted by women who consider themselves feminists, show that boys are more aggressive than girls for reasons that flow from biology, not environment. Research conducted during the past thirty years has also established that men's and women's brains are wired very differently, that we tend to specialize in different areas, and that sex differences in empathy, verbal fluency, and spatial ability all tell us something about why males are more likely to be violent than females.

Male physiology is another biological sex difference that enables men to inflict greater violence than women. Men are faster, stronger, and larger than women. We have less body fat, greater strength, and greater size. Many studies of domestic violence have found that on average, women hit their male partners almost as often as men hit their female partners. But the difference is in the consequences. Women may be just as likely to strike out in anger, but they are not likely to inflict anything like the harm that men can inflict. Male biology allows men to do more harm than women. And male anatomy—specifically, the penis—facilitates sexual assault.

Third, some men are biologically predisposed to violence in a way that other men are not. The early history of the biology of crime was an embarrassment—hence, there is a reluctance among academics to accept this connection. In the 19th century Cesare Lombroso concocted the idea that physical features could be related to criminality—the size and shape of a man's ears, the slope of his forehead, and so on. But no empirical validity has ever been forthcoming. William Sheldon expanded upon this silliness in the 20th century, suggesting that body type and criminality could be related; again, there is no empirical validity to this idea.

In the past generation, however, there has been more sophisticated research, with more compelling findings. Studies of adopted children in Denmark, Vietnam, and Sweden have uncovered the fact that a boy is more likely to obtain a criminal conviction if his biological father, not his adoptive father, has a criminal conviction.

In other words, the influence of biology on an individual's participation in criminal activity appears to be more significant than the influence of environment. Further, studies of fraternal and identical twins have established a genetic link between crime and individual biology: the closer the genetic link, the more likely there are to be similar patterns of criminal behaviour, even when fraternal and identical twins have been raised apart.

The fourth biological component in male violence is testosterone. Although testosterone is most closely related to male sexuality, it has a strong, albeit indirect, relationship to male violence. The postpuberty testosterone surge is highly correlated with a rapid surge in violent conduct by young men. The confusion, misunderstanding, and disappointments of adolescent sexuality can be seen in increased rates of criminal aggression.

We must begin to approach the problem of male violence with a more balanced diagnosis of the difficulties that we face. Our solutions will, for the most part, be located in a greater cultural and environmental awareness—in constructing a social world that can help us to respond to the inevitable risks of male violence. We must be sure that we diagnose this problem correctly; the world is more complex than cultural apologists would have us believe. Men are different from women in ways that ultimately threaten the survival of the species. And as long as we continue to misunderstand this problem of male aggression, we will continue to suffer from its consequences.

Chapter Two
The Evolution of Male Violence

We are not completed as we stand, this is not our final stage.
There can be no finished form for us or for anything else alive,
anything that travels from generation to generation. The Book of Life
is still being written. The end of the story is not predestined.

JONATHAN WEINER, THE BEAK OF THE FINCH

My own introduction to male violence began in New York City in the summer of 1964, when I was 12 years old, travelling with my aunt, uncle, and cousins. We checked into the venerable St. James Hotel, just off Times Square. My cousin Warren and I had both been raised in small towns, and we could not stop watching the action on the street from our eighth-storey window. My aunt, a teacher of contemporary American history, had requested a room directly across from the Peppermint Lounge, where Chubby Checker had recently launched a dance called the twist.

A few minutes before midnight Warren and I watched as a man bolted from the Peppermint Lounge and began running down the sidewalk. He was quickly followed out the door by another man, who stopped almost as soon as he left the lounge, raised his arm, and fired a gun at the man running down the street. The man running suddenly collapsed on the sidewalk, struck dead by a single bullet. Within minutes police cars and ambulances were arriving and my aunt and uncle were closing the windows and pulling Warren and me away from the most gripping spectacle we had ever witnessed.

But split that screen for a moment with a different image. It is 7:00 A.M. on a December day in 1999, on the beach at Hanalei Bay in Kauai, the northern tip of the archipelago known as the Hawaiian Islands. The sunlight is filtered by clouds massing along the ridge that curves behind the bay. On this morning there are about a dozen men, walkers and joggers, scattered along the 3-kilometre stretch of golden sand, some with their dogs, and some early risers with their morning coffee. There is a lot of friendly nodding when strangers pass each other. Lush vegetation and six-million-year-old rocky ridges frame the scattering of homes and cottages that line Weke Road and the ocean beyond. We are in the lap of civilized luxury. This place is as beautiful and serene as one can imagine, as kind and gentle as America can be.

But the idyllic calm of Hanalei is deceptive. Even this vacation paradise has a relatively recent history of violence, men killing, raping, and maiming other men and women.

The Hawaiian islands have the shortest duration of human settlement of any place on earth. About fifteen hundred years ago Polynesians arrived by outrigger canoes from Tahiti, settling on the eight major islands. They were the Kanaka Maoli, the native

Hawaiians, and by the mid-1700s there were about one million of them spread across the chain.

Each island was essentially a feudal state, ruled by chiefs and priests. Despite the bounty of their land, the Kanaka Maoli did not live in a state of peaceful bliss. There were constant battles for control of each island and for control of neighbouring islands. When European explorers arrived on the islands during the 18th century, King Kamehameha was emerging as the undisputed leader of the Hawaiian chain. The king solidified his hold on power in 1791 when he asked his adversary, Chief Kauwe, to come to Kona to talk. When Chief Kauwe and his under chiefs stepped ashore they were, apparently to their surprise, hacked to death on the beach. One biography of Kamehameha describes the scene:

> As Kamehameha's men cheered, Kauwe's body was taken up to the massive, stone Heiau overlooking Kawaihae Bay and offered up to Ku. Kauwe's flesh was ceremoniously stripped from his bones and eaten raw. This act transferred Kauwe's mana (spiritual and physical strengths) to those who partook in this act of cannibalism, as was the custom. . . . a fitting end to a worthy adversary and a festivity customarily reserved for family and friends.

When European explorers arrived, these patterns of violence intensified, thanks to technogical innovations in weaponry. Kamehameha was able to use the muskets and cannons brought by Captain James Cook and others, mounting these new weapons on his oceangoing war canoes to ensure his continued dominance of the archipelago. Besides guns, alcohol, and tobacco, the Europeans provided the Polynesians with gonorrhea, syphilis, and tuberculosis. During the next hundred years the population of the original Hawaiians was decimated by violence and disease. Although the Hawaiian monarchy remained in place until the late 1880s, British and American entrepreneurs began to take over the land. In 1893 Queen Liliuokalani was deposed by a group of American businessmen, acting with the support of American marines, and in 1898 President McKinley signed a resolution annexing Hawaii to the United States of America.

Under American control, the centuries-old legacy of violence and tribal conflict has continued. Japan bombed Pearl Harbor in 1941. Hawaii officially became a state of the United States in 1959, and in the years since then violence has continued, with lethal American engagements in Vietnam, Cambodia, Grenada, and Iraq.

The history of Hawaii is just one example from the whole human history of violence. In fact, that history begins before the appearance of human beings on the planet.

From Apes to Human Beings: A Common Thread

The late 20th century has provided us with a remarkable amount of evidence about human evolution. There is now consensus that human beings first emerged in central Africa as an offshoot of apes; our closest relatives are orangutans, gorillas, chimpanzees, and pygmy chimpanzees, also known as bonobos.

Our hominoid ancestors began to diverge from gorillas and orangutans about three or four million years ago, long before those ancestors diverged from chimpanzees. We are more like chimps than the gorillas are: we share 98.4 per cent of our DNA with chimpanzees; gorillas and orangutans share less of our DNA and less of the DNA of chimpanzees. Thus, chimpanzees are our closest relatives.

One attribute that clearly distinguishes us from chimpanzees and other apes is bipedal movement—the consistent practice of walking upright. Fossilized remains of skeletons indicate that about four million years ago there was a species that walked in the manner we walk. Fossil evidence also suggests that by two million years ago an ape now known as *Homo erectus* was multiplying rapidly, pushing into Europe and the Far East, leaving behind stone tools and bones. The brain size of this species continued to increase, and the skull became rounder. About 500,000 years ago our Cro-Magnon ancestors began to resemble us physically, having only slightly thicker skulls and more pronounced foreheads than we do today.

From 500,000 years ago to the end of the Ice Age, 40,000 years ago, there were two dominant types of primitive humans: the Cro-Magnons and the Neanderthals. The Neanderthals became extinct. Fossil evidence tells us that there were not as many Neanderthals as Cro-Magnons, and Neanderthals rarely lived past 40 years of age. Cro-Magnons often lived to 60, however, allowing for greater transmission of information across generations. Neanderthal tools were simpler than Cro-Magnon tools, and as a consequence, Neanderthals were much less accomplished hunters.

Cro-Magnons developed weapons—snares, and spears with sophisticated tips—but they also created paintings, ceramic sculptures, and musical instruments. We can only imagine what happened when Cro-Magnons and Neanderthals came upon each other, as they must have some forty or fifty thousand years ago. Like the Western Europeans who went to Hawaii in the late 18th century, the Cro-Magnons had technological advantages that would have overwhelmed the Neanderthals; one can imagine recurring cycles of invasion, violent death, and disease.

It is only in the last thirty years that researchers have started to observe the violence of apes other than ourselves in a systematic fashion. In the 1960s the predominant view of our closest relatives—chimpanzees—was that of a peaceful ape, living in harmony with nature. The celebrated science writer Robert Ardrey once wrote of their "arcadian existence of primal innocence."

Primatologist Richard Wrangham and writer Dale Peterson present evidence in *Demonic Males: Apes and the Origins of Human Violence* to demonstrate that orangutans, gorillas, chimpanzees, and human beings have all practised—and continue to practise—lethal aggression. Systematic observations in the wild and in captivity have altered our view of this lost Eden. Wrangham and Peterson describe a raid by one group of chimpanzees on an elderly member of another group:

> One year later, a gang from Kasekela found their third victim. This time the target was Goliath, now well past his prime, with a bald head, very worn teeth, protruding ribs and spine. He may have been well into his fifties. It was many years since he had last competed for dominance. He had been a well-integrated member of the Kasekela community only five years before, and now (though he had since joined the Kahama group) he was little threat to anyone. But none of that mattered to the aggressors.

It began as a border patrol. At one point they sat still on a ridge, staring down into Kahama Valley for more than three-quarters of an hour, until they spotted Goliath, apparently hiding only 25 meters away. The raiders rushed madly down the slope to their target. While Goliath screamed and the patrol hooted and displayed, he was held and beaten and kicked and lifted and dropped and bitten and jumped on. At first he tried to protect his head, but soon he gave up and lay stretched out and still. His aggressors showed their excitement in a continuous barrage of hooting and drumming and charging and branch-waving and screaming. They kept up the attack for 18 minutes, then turned for home, still energized, running and screaming and banging on tree-root buttresses. Bleeding freely from his head, gashed on his back, Goliath tried to sit up but fell back shivering. He too was never seen again.

This scene of a group of chimpanzees viciously destroying a perceived competitor or an individual from another group has countless recent human parallels: a gang of teenagers "swarming" a victim and kicking him to death, the murder of a young Somalian by Canadian soldiers in Africa, "ethnic cleansing" in the former Yugoslavia, acts of genocide in Rwanda, Uganda, Cambodia, East Timor, Burundi, Indonesia, Brazil, Sudan, and Bangladesh.

The human ape left Africa and gradually spread across the world, moving by land into climatically hospitable regions of Europe and Asia about a million years ago, before emerging as Cro-Magnon man. From that point onward, travel to more northern climates and travel by water became possible: human beings gradually moved into Siberia and from there to North and South America and finally on to Australia, New Zealand, and Hawaii. It was during the last forty thousand years that the characteristics of human beings that distinguish us from other primates began to emerge—art in the form of cave paintings; sophisticated weapons in the form of darts, spears, snares, and traps; and densely populated human settlements of homes, with fire as a means of heat.

It's difficult to understand how we transformed ourselves; there is no evidence of a written language until about 5,000 years ago. First evidence of the wheel occurs about 3,300 B.C., and there is some evidence of food production just a little before this time. But there is no evidence at that time that animals were used for their milk, their coats, or their labour. By today's standards, the first 35,000 years of Cro-Magnon life were remarkably primitive; it is only in the last 5,000 years that researchers can document a significantly developed capacity for analysis and reflection—within the passage of a mere two hundred generations of human beings.

Like chimpanzees, gorillas, and orangutans, humans have always been violent. Human beings, like gorillas, kill the young of their adversaries. Like male orangutans, male human beings rape. And like our closest relative, the chimpanzee, we practise intergroup destruction. Consider the following passage from Wrangham and Peterson's *Demonic Males* and note the striking similarity of chimpanzee conduct to any number of human military or civilian atrocities within the past decade. Wrangham and Peterson are describing the final obliteration of the Kahama group of chimpanzees by the Kasekela tribe.

One by one the six adult males of the Kahama community disappeared, until by the middle of 1977 an adolescent named
Sniff, around 17 years old, was the lone defender. Sniff, who as
a youngster in the 1960s had played with the Kasekela males,
was caught late on November 11. Six Kasekela males screamed
and barked in excitement as they hit, grabbed and bit their victim viciously—wounding him in the mouth, forehead, nose,
and back and breaking one leg. Goblin struck the victim repeatedly in the nose. Sherry, an adolescent just a year or two
younger than Sniff, punched him. Satan grabbed Sniff by the
neck and drank the blood streaming down his face. Then Satan
was joined by Sherry, and the two screaming males pulled
young Sniff down a hill. Sniff was seen one day later, crippled,
almost unable to move. After that he was not seen and presumed dead. By the end of 1977 Kahama was no more.

Horrifying as these events were, the most difficult aspect to
accept was not the physical unpleasantness but the fact that
the attackers knew their victims so well. They had been close
companions before the community split.

The similarity between the violence of chimpanzees and human beings is remarkable. Most killers know their victims well,
and lethal attacks are overwhelmingly male, motivated by real or
imagined provocation or the perceived need to annihilate a real or
imagined threat. Wrangham and Peterson argue, however, against
human violence as an evolutionary inevitability. They suggest that
there is another road that we might travel—that of the bonobos.

The Lessons of the Bonobos

Unlike the larger chimpanzees and human beings, the bonobos have fashioned a peaceful existence for themselves. There is no evidence of rape, infanticide, or lethal aggression by competing bands of males. The bonobos live in a relatively small area of Africa, just south of the Zaire River. They are marginally smaller than most chimpanzees, but male bonobos, like other apes, are slightly larger and stronger than female bonobos. Like chimpanzees, the bonobos travel in relatively small communities, sharing a range with about eighty others. Bonobo sons have an unusually close relationship with their mothers; they stay with them throughout their lives, travelling in the same party.

What is most striking about the bonobos is how often they engage in sex—and how varied their sexuality is. The females of the group typically engage in sex with each other (a rubbing of genitals called *hoka-hoka,* which appears to lead to orgasm); the males engage in sex with each other and with the females; there are manual manipulations of genitalia, oral-genital contact, and a wide variety of copulatory positions. Moreover, the bonobos have proportionately large genitalia relative to human beings and can mate several times each day. They also begin sexual contact long before the onset of puberty—activity that we would regard as criminal.

Bonobos appear to have little aggression between the sexes, among males of their groupings, or between communities. There are challenges to authority, but these challenges (usually initiated by males) do not result in any serious injury and are typically quelled by a closely knit group of female bonobos. Data from observations near the village of Wamba in Zaire have led Wrangham to conclude that female power is the key to managing male aggression. Wrangham has described a typical incident in one group of bonobos, observed and documented in a 1992 publication by Japanese primatologist Takayoshi Kano, demonstrating the lasting consequences of female intervention.

Kano observed the son of one of the group's most powerful females, Aki, charging Ude, the second-ranking male in the tribe. Aki's son, who was a young adult, was screaming and dragging a branch as he raced towards the older male. At the last moment he veered away from Ude. Annoyed by this insolence, Ude slapped the young male. The top-ranking male in the group intervened to prevent Ude from doing further harm. Undeterred by the slap in the face, Aki's son charged again. The two began to fight, kicking and hitting each other and screaming.

At this point Aki joined the fray, carrying her screaming baby on her belly. She chased Ude away more than ten times, and other females supported her with calls and gestures. Within a few hours Ude fled, and ten years after that single incident Kano reports that Ude remains subordinate to Aki's son, either fleeing or taking steps away whenever the two come into contact.

This example of female power has a human parallel in the black underclass of the United States, specifically within large urban centres between 1950 and the present, in what is referred to as "an exceptional sex ratio" in homicides. In cities such as Philadelphia and Detroit, black women are slightly more likely than black men to kill their spouses. Martin Daly and Margo Wilson suggest that this exception to the rule of killings by men can be explained by the presence of strong "matrilineal kinship networks," which again are parallel to the strong relationships among female bonobos. In impoverished inner-city neighbourhoods, where women with children live nearer to and have more frequent contact with their own kin than with their husbands', it is socially safer and more acceptable to retaliate against the coercive and violent behaviour of their male partners.

Wrangham and Peterson argue that the bonobos offer an alternative to global destruction by legion after legion of alpha male human apes. They also suggest that factors leading to the divergence of bonobos from human apes and other chimpanzees some 1.5 to 3 million years ago have resulted in the more peaceful nature of bonobos. It is fairly certain that gorillas and bonobos lived both north and south of the Zaire River about 8 million years ago. Gorillas eat fibrous foods, searching for leaves and stems on the forest floor, whereas bonobos eat fruit. During the ice ages, droughts in Africa eliminated the moist forests south of the Zaire River, and the gorillas were forced to move to the forested mountains to the north of the river.

After gorillas disappeared from the shores south of the Zaire River and the ice ages ended, restoring moisture to the planet, a more abundant food supply fell to the bonobos. They now had not only their traditional supply of fruit but also gorilla foods to eat—the leaves and stems of the forest floor. This abundance of food, according to Wrangham and Peterson, allowed larger and more socially stable parties of bonobos to travel and forage together. The community size of the bonobos, fuelled by this relative abundance of food, provided the conditions under which stable female relationships could be developed. Wrangham and Peterson's conclusion from all of this, set out in their 1996 book, is that there is no bio-logical inevitability to male violence. They point to the relatively peaceful bonobos and suggest that males, whether bonobos or human beings, are not biologically pre-ordained to aggress and destroy.

The Wrangham and Peterson thesis is based on a good deal of speculation, however. It is possible that the relative isolation of the bonobos either flows from or has led to very slight genetic differences that de-emphasize male violence. It is not certain why gorillas are not found south of the Zaire River; researchers require dry excavation sites to find an archaeological record of our relatives, and these are not available. Further, it is not certain that the relative abundance of food produced the development of female affiliations among the bonobos. Most important, no firm conclusions can be drawn from observations of a relatively small encampment of these apes in a relatively small part of the African continent in the 20th century.

The Human Response to Our Ape Ancestors

The bonobos aside, the historical record tells us that male violence has been a part of every ape culture of which we have knowledge. But these similarities in the way that we all live and the violence that we engage in are rarely the focus of our interest in other apes. We want to know instead how the other apes respond to viruses and to surgery. Knowledge of these apes as social beings takes a back seat to a more selfish question: How can we use the chimpanzee, gorilla, or orangutan to improve our physical health? In placing chimpanzees and the other apes in cages and forcing them to be guinea pigs for a wide range of scientific experiments, we human beings continue to diminish the humanity of these "lesser" primates—and, most important in the context of this book, we fail to see the extraordinarily common thread linking ape violence to human violence.

In the world of critical thinkers and humanists, even among those who consider themselves "progressives," the idea that we are similar to other primates is viewed with suspicion. These are folks who believe that human beings are distinctly different from apes, capable of reflection and analysis that differentiate us from the "lower" mammals. In their devotion to this model of separation for understanding human behaviour, some of these so-called progressives have advertently or inadvertently justified the murder and experimental abuse of thousands of highly intelligent primates.

For example, the American linguist Noam Chomsky has built his career on the notion that human beings have an inbuilt "language acquisition device" that no other primates can aspire to. There is no evidence in physiology or psychology for the existence of such a device, but Chomsky continues to mine his long-held theoretical claim. In the interim, a host of research studies has established the conceptual complexity of chimpanzee and human-chimpanzee communication.

In *Next of Kin: My Conversations with Chimpanzees,* his moving tribute to the chimpanzees that he has lived with for more than thirty years, Roger Fouts writes of his bittersweet reunion with Booee, a 27-year-old chimpanzee who had been sent to a scientific laboratory at age 13 and injected with hepatitis C. Booee was housed in a cage measuring 5 feet by 6 feet by 6 feet; there was no access to the outdoors and no windows.

A big smile lit up Booee's face. He remembered me, after all.

Hi, Booee, I signed. *You remember?*

Booee, Booee, Me Booee, he signed back, overjoyed that someone had actually acknowledged him. He kept drawing his finger down the center of his head in his name sign—the one I had given him in 1970, three years after National Institute of Health researchers had split his infant brain in two.

Yes, You Booee, You Booee, I signed back.

Give me food, Roger, he pleaded.

Booee not only remembered that I always carried raisins for him, but he used the nickname he had invented for me twenty-five years earlier. Instead of tugging the ear lobe for ROGER, he flicked his finger off the ear. This was like calling someone "Rodg" instead of "Roger." Seeing him sign my old nickname floored me. I had forgotten it, but Booee hadn't. He remembered the good old days better than I did.

I gave Booee some raisins and the years just melted away, the way they do between old friends. He reached his hand through the bars and groomed my arm. He was happy again. He was the same sweet boy I met on that autumn day decades earlier. . . . I was a young know-it-all professor then, right out of graduate school. I yelled at Booee one day, and he humbled me in front of my very first college students by lifting me off my feet and letting me dangle there. For twenty-five years I'd been telling students about how Booee embraced me and forgave my anger toward him.

Look at him now, I thought. Thirteen years in a hellhole and he's still forgiving, still guileless. Booee still loved me, in spite of everything that humans had done to him. How many people would be so generous of spirit?

I must go now, Booee, I signed after a while. Booee's grin changed to a grimace, and his body sank. *I must leave, Booee.* Booee moved to the back of his cage. *Good-bye, Booee.*

The History of Human Violence

Archaeological evidence tells us that male *Homo sapiens* have always been violent; the written record of the past five thousand years confirms this consistent pattern of behaviour. From the archaeological record of nomadic peoples to the written records of the Sumerians of Mesopotamia, Athenian Greece, the Roman Empire, the Dark Ages, and the Renaissance, up to the global empires and the world wars of the recent past, male violence has been a ubiquitous underpinning of political and social organization.

There are different kinds of male violence, however, and some cultures have experienced a good deal more of this affliction than others. There is first and always some amount of violence at the level of the family—the phenomenon of killing among intimates. Most commonly, a man assaults, injures, or kills his wife or lover, kin, or former friend; this form of violence has existed in every society, past and present.

As societies have become larger and more complex, the extent of male violence has concomitantly increased. The simplest form of living arrangement, which began in our evolutionary past, was the band of primates. Originally, dozens of men and women lived together in a nomadic existence, and any male member of the group might use force to resolve disagreements. Violence among kin was relatively common, and it still is among gorillas, chimpanzees, and orangutans that live in the wild.

Even twenty years ago the Fayu band of New Guinea was continuing its tradition of violence. In the late 1970s the Fayu lived nomadically in a remote swamp of New Guinea, four hundred huntergatherers wandering over a few hundred square miles. Whenever a group of Fayu came together, murder was a distinct possibility, an opportunity to avenge previous killings of close relatives. With no mechanisms for dispute resolution and no centralized system of political authority, male violence was the medium of negotiation. In the past decade missionaries have lived with the Fayu, gradually persuading them to reject violence.

The human band expanded and evolved into the tribe when a hospitable climate, farming, and the herding of animals made fixed settlements possible. The tribe was characterized by hundreds of men and women living in the relatively fixed settlement of a village; again, any male could use force in such societies. But conflict now arose between neighbouring villages; male violence was directed not only towards the family but also towards an outside threat, real or perceived.

The tribe gradually evolved into what anthropologists and others have termed a chiefdom, a collection of thousands of individuals, often ruled by a hereditary chief with centralized political power. In this construction, the chief asserted a monopoly on the use of force. Decision making was no longer egalitarian but hierarchical and was typically based on heredity. Again, violence did not disappear with the advent of the chiefdom. Chiefdoms in conflict with each other were, in many important respects, functionally similar to tribes in conflict with each other. And by the standards of contemporary Western democracies, chiefdoms, or what might also be termed early states, were brutally violent societies.

In many parts of the world, the chiefdom and the early state society have typically evolved into the most common of our current forms of political organization, the modern state. This state, like the chiefdom or the early state, has a monopoly on the use of force and centralized decision making. Unlike the chiefdom, however, conflicts are now mediated through democratic elections and the rule of law rather than through pronouncements from a hereditary elite. One of the advantages of the modern state is that having a centralized monopoly of force can serve to maintain public order and diminish the potential for individual acts of violence.

The transition of societies from the band to the modern state is not a simple linear progression. The Fayu, a band of nomads, still live in a remote part of New Guinea. And even the presence of democracy and the rule of law does not always act as a brake on male violence. The Romans, who established at least a rudimentary form of democracy, permitted fathers to exile, torture, and kill their children. Edward Gibbon reports in *The Decline and Fall of the Roman Empire* that men were never punished and were sometimes praised for such killings.

In 13th-century England a panel of royal justices travelled about the country, hearing all forms of actions, including criminal claims, in a court known as the Eyre. Surviving records indicate that in most English counties—for example, in Bedford, Warwick, Oxford, and Kent—the rate of homicide was about ten times as high as it is today in the same locations.

The character of homicide was also very different from the character of homicide in England today. Almost 75 per cent of killings were undertaken by a group rather than a single individual. These groups were almost universally male and ranged from two to four individuals to twenty or more. Moreover, these lethal exchanges typically involved kinship groups or individuals with close social ties. A group of villagers or a clan of family members would band together to attack a victim or victims. The parallels with the Kasekela and Kahama tribes are striking. Like chimpanzees at their worst, human beings at their worst have consistently engaged in intergroup raiding.

This kind of behaviour continued in England, from all accounts, until the late 1700s. Angry mobs would set upon men or women they considered to be deserving of punishment and beat and kick them to death. The system of justice was violent. Petty thieves—both men and women—were dragged through local towns tied to the back of a cart and whipped, often to the point of debilitating injury. Others were placed in a wooden pillory in the town square, their hands and head locked in the heavy structure. In many instances, again, an angry crowd beat these people to death, or threw objects that led to death or serious injury. Women were burned at the stake for treason and for killing their abusive husbands. The death penalty was imposed for an array of offences, from adultery to theft to robbery and homicide. Men who were defined as traitors, pretenders to the throne of the alpha male, received the most vicious treatment. The traitor was usually hanged, cut down while still alive, and then castrated and disembowelled, beheaded, and cut into quarters.

During the past three centuries, in Western Europe and North America, physical violence has diminished strikingly in daily life; the nature and extent of homicide has also changed. At the same time, however, pockets of extreme violence remain. For example, in Cleveland, Ohio, between 1969 and 1974, the rate of homicide among black males was more than 150 times as high as the rate of homicide in England or Japan and about 15 times as high as the rate of homicide elsewhere in the United States. If the state's monopoly on the use of force is not respected, male violence can be as common and as brutal as among New Guinea's Fayu.

But although violence has remained largely a male institution, killings in most Western industrialized democracies have become less common, less of a group phenomenon, and more likely to be attributed to the actions of a single individual. This is a significant advantage for any community, but the rise of the modern state does appear to have created a new problem, with the possibility of even greater injury and loss of life.

In the 19th and 20th centuries, despite global knowledge of the costs of violence and the social benefits of democratic government and peaceful coexistence, the incidence of genocide among chiefdoms and nation-states has increased. As Jared Diamond has pointed out, between 1950 and 1990 the world has seen six instances of genocide with more than 10,000 victims, four instances of genocide with more than 100,000 victims, and two instances with more than 1 million victims—the killings during the 1970s by the Khmer Rouge and the Pakistani army.

Genocides of unprecedented proportions have also been made possible because populations have increased and our technologies of killing have improved, thanks to continuing advances in communications and weaponry. The future that we are constructing on this planet cannot easily be seen as hopeful. Although the development of democratic states has diminished the potential for individual violence, the possibility of global annihilation has simultaneously increased. In the face of greater knowledge of the costs of violence, men continue to impose even greater harm on their fellow human beings.

Minoan Crete and Mead's New Guinea

There have been challenges to the idea that human history is an unbroken string of male dominance and lethal attack. The Minoan civilization, lasting from 6000 B.C. to 1500 B.C., has been described as a time when male violence was silenced. The Minoan culture was marked by slow and steady technological progress in pottery making, weaving, metallurgy, engraving, architecture, and other crafts, and the many goddess images that have been recovered from archaeological excavations stand in stark contrast to images of war or battle created by subsequent generations.

But weaponry from this era has also been found in Crete— and there is evidence of the destruction by fire of several sites in Phaistos Mallia, Vasiliki, and Gournia. This evidence suggests communities in conflict, practising the ritual of intercommunity aggression and annihilation. There is also evidence in Crete of human sacrifice.

So the image of Minoan Crete as a matriarchal haven of peace and tranquillity may be exaggerated, though there remains a hopefulness in the images and artifacts of this culture. Although male dominance and violence were probably features of this age, other features point to a more life-affirming, more artistic, and less violent existence than those that followed.

In the past century, however, hundreds of thousands of college students have been taught outright fabrications—Margaret Mead's studies of the "gentle" Arapesh and Tschambuli tribes in New Guinea, documented in two highly successful books in the 1930s. The books suggested that sex differences between men and women are entirely the product of culture and, as a consequence, are easily reversible. Mead insisted that both male and female Arapesh were gentle and passive and that among Tschambuli women "we found a genuine reversal of the sex-attitudes of our culture," meaning that the women were typically dominant. Although Mead never presented any specific observational data to support her contentions and contradicted herself by pointing to homicide in both cultures as a recurring phenomenon, the myth of her investigations lives on. Subsequent research has established that Arapesh men have a social obligation to commit a homicide in order to be initiated into adulthood. The Tschambuli also have a long history of warfare, having totally destroyed several neighbouring tribes. In both cultures violence is an activity engaged in almost exclusively by men.

Over the last century, there has been a desire to idealize the past—to believe that the lives of various First Nations bands and tribes were gentle and nonviolent, even spiritually transcendent. But detailed research that has catalogued the long-term behaviours of band and tribal societies—such as the Fayu, the Arapesh, and the native Hawaiians—often contradicts such claims. We may want to believe in the more peaceful Eden of a simpler society, but there are no data and no logic to support such a hypothesis.

Finally, it must be acknowledged that in even the most war-torn of bands, tribes, communities, or nation-states, social life is not an unbroken string of predatory barbarism—and this is as true today as it appears to have been five thousand or forty thousand years ago. Men and women make love, raise children, and in most circumstances live their lives relatively peacefully, typically free from the threat of lethal attack. But male violence appears, even in the most peaceful of cultures, as an overarching constant, a ghost in the rear-view mirror.

Male Violence and the Search for Sex

Evolutionary biologists and psychologists take these facts and make an argument that goes one step further. They suggest that the consistency of male violence can be explained by natural selec-tion: the survival of organisms that are best able to adapt to the en-vironment in which they find themselves.

J. W. Tutt observed that in the industrial pollution of 19th-century Britain the more darkly coloured moths tended to predom-inate over lighter-coloured moths; dark colours enabled moths to blend in with the soot-covered bark on trees and thus to escape detection by predators. This adaptation to their environment made the reproduction and survival of this type of moth more likely. Sim-ilarly, the peacock's tail, though it is a colourful invitation to preda-tors, also conveys an enticing message to female peacocks. The colourful tail has survived, not because it produces longevity for any given peacock, but because it has been successful in attracting mates, thereby increasing the potential for reproduction and the survival of the species.

Evolutionary psychologists and biologists argue that male violence is like the dark moth or the peacock's tail. In the absence of social constraints, violent men are more likely to impregnate women than nonviolent men are, more likely to reproduce, and thus more likely to ensure the survival of violence as a social strategy within the species.

Biology dictates that women cannot produce as many heirs as men, who have the potential to produce hundreds, even thousands, of children in a lifetime. A male can always gain access to one more fertile female, regardless of whether he has a single mate or more than a hundred; the female, in contrast, is limited to sequential pregnancies to pass on her genes to the next generation.

In other words, male reproductive success is more variable than female reproductive success. Women can produce a range of heirs from zero to twenty or more; men can produce a range from zero to more than one thousand. And a more sexually driven male is more likely to impregnate a greater number of women than a male who is less interested in sex.

The relationship between sexuality and violence is more complex. For violent men to be more likely to reproduce, they must first be strongly interested in sex; being violent is, in itself, not enough to propel their genes into the next generation. In societies that have few constraints on sexual aggression and violence, men who force themselves upon women are more likely to reproduce, thus perpetuating sexual aggression and violence within the species.

But there is evidence that violence in itself can be counter-productive to the survival of a group of individuals. The nomadic Fayu of New Guinea once numbered about two thousand, but constant violence among the men of the band has reduced their numbers to a little more than four hundred. Similarly, when the nine mutineers from the HMS *Bounty* arrived on Pitcairn Island in 1790, with six Polynesian men and thirteen Polynesian women, they set about building a life in which competition for the women produced constant conflict. When Pitcairn was discovered about eighteen years later, only one man and ten women remained alive. Violence, driven by competition for the thirteen Polynesian women, was reducing the survivability of the species.

The point is not that sexual competition flows from a sexually violent male's conscious intent to pass on his genes to the next generation. After all, it has only been within the last few thousand years that human beings have drawn a connection between sexual intercourse and its consequences. All we can say for certain is that men, from their origins in Africa to the present, have always wanted sex. There is a simple reason for this: sex is very pleasurable—and, all other things being equal, more sexually aggressive and violent men are more likely to be able to obtain more sex.

In societies that have few constraints on sexual violence, men who have the greatest amount of unprotected sex with the greatest number of partners—and hence who are most likely to produce the greatest number of offspring—are the most sexually aggressive of males. But these offspring need a supportive and nurturing environment to survive and to reproduce themselves. In Western industrial societies today, child welfare and protection agencies can supply some of this support if it is missing at home. But in earlier societies and in some societies today, this support must come from the family. If it is not there, children are less likely to survive and flourish. Thus, the characteristics of a sexually violent man might lead to pregnancy and birth, but they also tend to discourage the survival of offspring and hence to work against population growth.

In Western cultures other factors determine who reproduces and which offspring survive: religious beliefs, moral convictions, education, health care, birth control, and income, among others. In the early 21st century in the United States and Canada, birth rates are highest in the most impoverished—and most violent—sectors of the community. The middle class—with better knowledge and control of reproduction, a desire to limit family size, and the ability to plan for economic goals—is typically much less prolific. And the children of sexually violent men can usually count on stability and support from the rest of their family or from social organizations. The centralized state will help ensure that they survive infancy and live to reproduce. Thus, our humane commitment to prop up the most vulnerable among our population also works, albeit inadvertently, to perpetuate the sexually violent male.

The Unpacified Male

Robert Wright, the author of *The Moral Animal,* argues further that it is dangerous for a society to have a lot of men who have neither wives nor children. He suggests that violence is especially ferocious among these "unpacified men." The man who has no community of reference will allow a trivial disagreement to escalate into a physical confrontation to win some measure of self-respect for himself.

There are data to support Wright's thesis. Married men are much less likely to be murder suspects than single men; they generally have more to lose from criminal conviction and imprisonment, both materially and emotionally, than do single men. Further, learning the give-and-take and the cooperation and compromise of partnership can often serve to "pacify"—to moderate a male's inclination to aggression and violence. Monogamous marriage and an extended family are key elements for the formation of a less violent society.

As Robert Wright argues:

A polygynous nation, in which large numbers of low-income men remain mateless, is not the kind of country many of us would want to live in. Unfortunately, this is the sort of country we already live in. The United States is no longer a nation of institutionalized monogamy. It is a nation of serial monogamy. . . . Johnny Carson, like many wealthy, high-status males, spent his career monopolizing long stretches of the reproductive years of a series of young women. Somewhere out there is a man who wanted a family and a beautiful wife and, if it hadn't been for Johnny Carson, would have married one of these women. And if this man has managed to find another woman, she was similarly snatched from the jaws of some other man. And so on— a domino effect: a scarcity of fertile females trickles down the social scale.

There are some important caveats to this statement. In our culture, where child care is not highly valued, it is the personal commitment of monogamy, in addition to a search for fertility, that is at the heart of social stability. Men who are in stable relationships with other men, and women who are in stable relationships with other women, will not reproduce, but they cannot be said to represent a greater order of risk for violence. And heterosexual partnerships of men and women who do not want to reproduce are not at greater risk of socially destructive behaviour than couples who can and do reproduce. But Robert Wright is correct in suggesting that relationships between men and women are at the heart of male violence—and that a society in which there are more committed partnerships is a society that is likely to be more peaceful.

Sexuality is at the very core of male violence. An elementary understanding of the principles of natural selection tells us that more sexually violent men are more likely to reproduce, in the absence of significant social constraints—and that even in the more socially constrained cultures in which we live in the early 21st century, sexually violent men are more likely to reproduce.

If we turn to the reasons for male violence, sexuality is once again at centre stage. The most common type of killing in our culture is that of a male killing his intimate partner, usually for reasons related to sexuality. The female victim has betrayed him by becoming involved with another man, by leaving him, or by failing to live up to his expectations. More than half of all killings in virtually every nation-state are perpetrated by a male against a female partner. When police are asked to describe the motivations for such crimes they document "anger," "jealousy," "hatred," and "revenge" as the critical factors. Further, other killings of family members, close friends, and business associates typically have their genesis in the failure or absence of an intimate relationship.

Sexuality has always been a focus for violence, from the bands and tribes of early humans to the present. A female anthropologist, interviewing women of New Guinea's Iyau tribe, learned that woman after woman had several husbands, all of whom had died violent deaths related to intimate relationships. For example, one woman noted that her second husband had been killed by a man who desired her; this man became her third husband. Her third husband was killed, in turn, by the brother of her second husband to avenge the earlier killing.

It is no accident that crime statistics in every culture point to young men as overwhelmingly responsible for violence and violent death. The single male, at his sexual peak, is vulnerable to all forms of conflict. (The critical contribution of testosterone to this phenomenon is discussed in chapter 5.) In all of the world's nation-states, violent-crime rates mirror levels of male sexual arousal. The age-crime curve for men rises sharply at age 15 and peaks at age 20, as sexual energy is similarly reaching its pinnacle. The twenties are marked by a precipitous decline in violence as young men find partners and social stability and begin their involvement in raising the next generation.

Zoologist and science writer Matt Ridley, writing in *The Red Queen* about polygamy and the nature of men, suggests that inter-community war and violence are less about territory and power than they are about sex. Ridley argues that war is something we have inherited directly from hostilities between groups of male apes over female apes and points to Venezuela's Yanomamo people as an example of this type of conflict. Among these people, two-thirds of those who reach the age of 40 have lost a close relative to murder.

Anthropologist Napoleon Chagnon travelled to Venezuela in the 1960s to find out what motivates the extraordinary violence among the Yanomamo. The Yanomamo told Chagnon that their disputes are about women, not territory or property. War between neighbouring villages breaks out over the abduction of a woman, or in retaliation for an attack that had as its goal such an abduction. The consequence of these attacks is most typically that a woman is passed from one male or group of males to another as the spoils of victory. Similarly, when there is violence within a village the most likely cause is sexual jealousy; a village that is very small appears likely to be raided for its women, and a village that is too large begins to tear itself apart because of adultery.

Ridley suggests that the history of violence may be best understood if it focuses on women as the reason for male conflict:

> The founding myth of western culture, Homer's *Iliad,* is a story
> that begins with a war over the abduction of a woman, Helen.
> Historians have long considered the abduction of Helen to Troy
> to be no more than a pretext for territorial confrontation be-
> tween the Greeks and the Trojans. But can we be so confidently
> condescending? . . . The *Iliad* opens with—and is dominated
> by—a quarrel between Achilles and Agamemnon, the cause of
> which is Agamemnon's insistence on confiscating a concubine.
> This dissension in the ranks, caused by a dispute over a woman,
> nearly loses the Greeks the whole war, which in turn has been
> caused by a dispute over a woman.

Ridley goes on to note that in prestate agricultural societies the captives taken in war were usually women, not men, and that victory was more likely to be motivated by the possibility of sexual conquest or rape than by community solidarity or fear. Similarly, in the present, West Pakistani troops raped almost half a million women during the 1970s, and in Bosnia in 1992 there were, again, countless reports of organized rape camps for the soldiers of Serbia. Anthropological and sociological evidence also suggests that the conversations of soldiers under siege are focused not on victory, territory, or domination of a foe but on sex and the pleasures that it might bring.

The Future of Male Violence

The birth control pill was one of the most revolutionary developments of the late 1960s and early 1970s. For the first time in history, women had reliable control over reproduction. As a partial result, the number of women in the labour force in North America and Europe more than doubled, altering the economic and hence political nature of the relationship between men and women. The divorce rate more than quadrupled after a generation of stability. The pill—and more effective treatment of sexually transmitted diseases—also permitted a polygamous sexuality, which coincided with a remarkable increase in the incidence of male violence. As female monogamy unravelled in the face of birth control in Europe and North America, rates of homicide more than doubled. The ability of women to control their reproductive freedom changed the rules of sexuality, and sexuality is at the core of male violence.

Our future does not look very bright. Male violence is no longer restrained by the biologically driven commitment of women to

monogamy. Further, there is a continuing tradition of male genocide in a dozen nation-states, where technologies of weaponry and
communications now produce millions of casualties instead of the
hundreds or thousands killed in previous centuries.

There are, admittedly, some marks of progress. There is less violence in Britain, Europe, and North America than there was three
hundred years ago—we live in imperfect democracies that do seem
to restrain male violence, albeit to markedly different degrees. The
future evolution of male violence is a process that we have at least
some potential to influence; the past three centuries in one limited
part of our world is proof of this possibility.

Studies on the Galápagos Islands over the last generation have
demonstrated that the evolution of many characteristics can take
place rapidly, not in the span of millions or even thousands of years,
but in the months of a single summer—the generational span of
finches. Jonathan Weiner's Pulitzer Prize–winning *Beak of the
Finch* documents the work of researchers on Daphne Major and
other islands. What emerges from the work of Peter and Rosemary
Grant and other scientists who have studied the finches of the
Galápagos is that the balance of survival is always shifting, dependent upon the availability of particular types of food, the physical
tools that the given finch has at its disposal, and the ever-changing
patterns of rain and drought. Weiner writes:

> The original meaning of the word evolution—the unrolling of a
> scroll—suggested a metamorphosis, as of moths or beetles or
> butterflies. But the insects' metamorphosis has a conclusion, a
> finished adult form. The Darwinian view of evolution shows

that the unrolling scroll is always being written, inscribed as it unrolls. The letters are composed by the hand of the moment, by the circumstances of the day itself. We are not completed as we stand, this is not our final stage. There can be no finished form for us or for anything else alive, anything that travels from generation to generation. The Book of Life is still being written. The end of the story is not predestined.

It is with this kind of optimism and duality that we must think of the future of male violence. In the often sweltering heat of the Galápagos, the scroll of Darwin's finches is unrolling itself, not in some inevitable path, following the dictates of genetic structure, but almost haphazardly, chaotically, the consequence of the finch's beak and the ever-changing environment of the islands.

And so it is with the future of male violence. Explanations for violence originate in biology, in male sexuality, and in the unfortunate predispositions of the male ape. If we want to understand and respond to this problem, we will have to recognize that in all important respects men are male apes. We no longer live in bands or tribes but in nation-states that carry their own risks of global annihilation. We have woven an unbroken thread of male violence into every band, tribe, and nation-state that has ever existed on the planet—and if we fail to recognize these origins as fundamentally biological, we will condemn ourselves to continue that legacy.

Chapter Three

Sex Differences and the Dark Heart of Political Correctness

*You'll notice that what they have in common is between
the legs. Is this why wars are fought?*

MARGARET ATWOOD, "A WOMEN'S ISSUE"

For more than twenty years my wife and I have lived on a small island off the coast of British Columbia. Much of Bowen was logged at the turn of the century, but it is now resplendent with the second growth of the Pacific Northwest rain forest. A mix of cedars, hemlock, and fir shares space with young alder and maple; the island is awash in different shades of green every spring. The summers are typical of the Pacific Northwest: warm, dry, and remarkably beautiful. The winters are not quite as beautiful: grey and rainy, but with a comforting domestic coziness.

As the population has grown, so has the load on the ferry that transports cars and people to Vancouver. Every morning the passenger deck is almost overflowing with the exuberant energy of children and teenagers travelling to schools in the city. It is almost always the boys who are the most physically active, most likely to wrestle with each other, to shout loudly to their friends, to throw things, to run from one end of the boat to the other, to leap into the air, to hip-check their friends into the wall, to push each other over the available seats—and to be disciplined by ferry staff or other adults. The girls, in contrast, are usually relatively sedate. They sit and talk with each other; they preen in the washroom; they roll their eyes as the boys fly by.

What causes these differences in behaviour? And why do little boys engage in rough-and-tumble play with trucks and balls while little girls engage in less rambunctious manipulations with dolls and kitchen toys? Many liberally minded academics and policymakers argue that these differences are entirely the consequence of social-ization: boys are physically forceful because they have been taught that boys should be physically forceful; girls are quiet and coopera-tive because they have been taught to be quiet and cooperative.

Sex Differences and Aggression

Science tells a different story. In the late 1980s researcher Diane McGuinness and her students watched thirty-eight boys and thirty-five girls, ages 3 to 5, play without supervision in their preschool. Even at that young age girls participated in only half as many physi-cal activities as boys, and boys were much more likely than girls to hit or push another child and to use a toy for some other purpose than that for which it was designed. This research finding has been corroborated in study after study, conducted by women who consider themselves feminists, using children who have been raised by parents who oppose sexual stereotypes. Although this evidence suggests that young boys are more aggressive than young girls for reasons that flow from biology, not culture, some people argue that young children, even at 2 or 3 years of age, pick up subtle sex-specific cues from their parents that encourage aggression or passivity, cooperation or competition.

But studies of congenital adrenal hyperplasia, usually referred to as CAH, make this explanation implausible. CAH is a condition in which female fetuses are exposed to very high levels of testosterone while in the womb. As a consequence of this hormonal bath, they often have ambiguous genitalia. Typically, their genitalia are repaired during infancy to look completely female and the children are always raised as girls.

These CAH girls, washed in male hormone before birth but raised as females, would seem a perfect test of the influence of biology. If environment is crucial, we would expect that many of these girls would exhibit "feminine" toy preferences and behave in most significant respects as little girls would behave. If, however, the bath in male hormone were more critical, we would expect these girls to have more "masculine" toy preferences and to behave in most significant respects as boys behave.

In the 1980s, psychologists Sheri Berenbaum and Melissa Hines set out to test the importance of environment on the toy preferences of CAH girls. Their subjects had all been correctly identified at birth as girls with congenital adrenal hyperplasia. The two researchers videotaped normal boys, CAH girls, and normal girls in a small area in which there was a range of toys available:

cars, trucks, blocks, dolls, kitchen toys, crayons, and paper. They found that the CAH girls and the boys spent more than half their time playing with the "boys' toys": cars, trucks, and blocks; correspondingly, the CAH girls spent less than half as much time playing with "girls' toys" as the normal girls did.

When the two researchers asked parents to fill out a questionnaire about how they raised their children, they could find no difference in responses; the behaviours and attitudes of the parents of the normal girls and the CAH girls were similar. A testosterone bath in the womb had a greater effect on toy preferences than the apparently more subtle cues of environment did.

Julianne Imperato-McGinley of Cornell Medical School studied thirty-eight men in Santo Domingo whose hormonal systems did not permit the formation of male genitalia at the time of birth. Quite mistakenly, these men were raised until puberty as females. At the onset of puberty their testicles descended, their clitorises became penises, and for all intents and purposes, they changed sex. McGinley's research, reported in *Science* in 1976, noted that after more than a decade of socialization as female, none of these thirty-eight men had any difficulty in assuming a male identity. The power of socialization again took a back seat to the power of testosterone.

The best evidence available suggests that sex differences in rough-and-tumble play and in choice of toys have more to do with biological difference than with sexism or the oppression of women. Those of us who came of age during the 1960s initially had a very different view of this matter, urging that the next generation be raised in a gender-neutral environment—dolls for boys, trucks for girls, no colour coding of clothing based on gender—so that any sexist behavioural differences between boys and girls could be eliminated. Further, most of the researchers in this area are women who strongly believe in gender equality. As psychologist Sheri Berenbaum has noted, when she started graduate school she really believed in the social environment, but her own research and the research of her colleagues has convinced her that biology plays a major role.

The experiences of my friends and acquaintances on Bowen Island are similar. I have watched their children grow from babies to young adults. These are folks who, like my wife and me, have endorsed and (I hope) retained the best of the ideals of the late 1960s: peace, tolerance, civility, and an end to sexism and racism. They have not wanted their boys to be raised to be aggressive or their girls to be passive or compliant; they reject the notion that toy preferences, sports, and the colour of clothing must be linked to the gender of their children. But they have seen that boys and girls are different, independent of any environmental influence.

However, to assert that some important differences in behaviour between men and women flow from biology is seen in some quarters as antifeminist and antifemale. To speak of sex differences is considered to be denying human potential and to be asserting that one sex is superior to the other. For example, the feminist biologist Anne Fausto-Sterling claims in her popular book, *Myths of Gender,* that those who find evidence of sex differences have an unconscious political agenda of female suppression.

My own experiences in academe confirm that Fausto-Sterling's comment has considerable support. In many North American universities, faculties of arts and social sciences are replete with ideologues who eschew conventional science, urging a "progressive feminist discourse" in opposition to the "hegemony" of the scientific method.

The study of sex differences is a sensitive issue for many folks in universities, who believe it is simply not appropriate to speak of sex differences in male and female abilities and sensibilities. The academic culture demands discussion and analysis of socially constructed "masculinities" and "femininities," rejecting talk of biological influences as regressive or reactionary. Although it is easy to dismiss this kind of thinking as irrelevant to anyone rooted in the real world (consider the Oxford dictionary's secondary definition of *academic:* "not of practical relevance"), remember that these folks write books and speak to millions of impressionable young people every day of the year; even the media consult them for their sage advice and counsel.

Some academics have tried to establish that contrary to the claims of many biologists, women can be just as aggressive as men. In an article published in *Psychological Bulletin* in 1986, psychologists Alice Eagly and Valerie Steffen of Purdue University focused on behavioural data relating to aggression. They included only studies that measured aggressive behaviour in experimental situations, looking to published work in Canada and the United States that documented sex differences in adolescent and adult populations.

In order to be included in their review, a research study had to measure aggressive behaviour directed towards another person and have a large enough sample size to permit calculation of the statistical significance of a sex difference. In field and laboratory settings subjects were given the opportunity to aggress in a variety of ways: giving an electric shock to subjects who showed poor heart rate control, honking at a bicyclist blocking the road, making unfriendly or rude gestures to an opinion surveyor, and commenting disapprovingly to a person cutting into line.

As Eagly and Steffen had predicted, men delivered and received more aggression than women. But the size of the sex difference in aggression was not what one might have expected from violent crime statistics. Although 90 per cent of convicted murderers are male, men are not nine times as likely as women to be aggressive. Some studies found no sex difference at all in the nature and extent of aggression, and some found that females were more aggressive than males. The authors concluded that the studies, taken as a group, indicate that men are not invariably more aggressive than women.

But there are two major difficulties with their line of argument. First and most important, they do not distinguish between aggression and violence. It is one thing to ask male and female subjects to administer an electric shock at a distance, to honk, or to make a rude gesture; it is quite another to commit violent acts such as assault, robbery, homicide, and sexual assault. It would be unethical to construct experiments in which such extreme behaviours would be triggered, but without such dependent variables in place, any claims about gender equality in the tendency to use physical aggression are without foundation.

Second, sex differences in aggression are usually much larger in studies of children than in studies of adults—a finding that raises questions about the roles of biological predisposition and socialization. Until they are provided with years of socialization, boys are much more aggressive and more violent than girls. At early ages, the limits of rough-and-tumble play have not yet been clearly defined and the structure of competitive sport has not been provided. The weight of the evidence indicates that young boys are biologically predisposed to aggression in a way that young girls are not. By the time boys become adults, most—but by no means all—have moderated their aggressive tendencies and are no more likely to use force than women. But the global overrepresentation of men in homicide statistics has its origins in the actions of boys on the grade school playground.

Size, Strength, and Speed

Imagine the world as a place where women are larger, faster, and stronger than men—the opposite of what we have always experienced. Would most prison inmates, prison guards, and police officers be female? Would men be referred to as "the gentler sex"? Perhaps men are more violent than women simply because we can be. On average, men are about 10 per cent taller, heavier, and faster than women and 35 per cent stronger; we also have half as much body fat. When push comes to shove, or worse, women are almost always more likely to be injured.

The point is not that women inevitably impose little harm or that they always occupy a moral high ground in relation to violence. Surveys of physical conflict between male and female partners reveal that women are almost as likely to be violent in these mutually abusive relationships. Like men, women can and do hit, punch, kick, stab, shoot, and strangle their victims. As Patricia Pearson has argued in *When She Was Bad: Violent Women and the*

Myth of Innocence, we must provide "shade and nuance" to the portrait of male and female violence:

> This has become an awkward paradox in feminist argument. How do we argue that we can be aggressive on every front—the Persian Gulf, the urban police beat, the empires of business, sports, hunting, politics, debate—but never in a manner that does harm?

The evidence that women can do harm, physically and emotionally, is clear and overwhelming. Consider Karla Homolka, who with her husband, Paul Bernardo, kidnapped, sexually assaulted, and murdered two teenage girls. (When caught, Homolka argued a traditional if unconvincing "feminist" line—that she, too, was a victim, and that she participated in violence as a result of "learned helplessness" and "battered women's syndrome.")

But male size, strength, and speed are almost always determining factors in male-female conflicts. For example, 16-year-old Sally Brennan might be alive today if she had been a little larger, stronger, and faster than Dirk Rochester. Superior size, strength, and speed were crucial to the success of his attack. Rochester described his motivation for the killing:

> I had this thing for a lot of years, a fixation for murder. . . . Mass murderers, single murderers, Ted Bundys. . . . all these type of people. And a lot of time when I'd go out and I'd be drunk or whatever, I'd just go out prowling around just looking for somebody to kill.

It was somebody that was so afraid of everything and so scared . . . you can tell that in people when you encounter them at four o'clock in the morning on the street. . . . You can tell if they're emotionally unstable . . . and that's what I was looking for.

Rochester killed Sally Brennan in a park; he simply overpowered her, squeezing life from her throat. There are many more examples of the same phenomenon in the more common realm of domestic homicides. Steve Galloway, very drunk and angry, strangled his wife, Brenda, in the late 1970s during a dispute about who should have driven the babysitter home. Peter Beyak was told by his wife in early 1933 that she had found a better man and wanted him to move out of their home. After three days of quarrelling, Beyak hit his wife with a meat cleaver. He described the killing to police, "We continued quarelling worse and worse until I went crazy, then that's all I could remember until I saw her lying on the floor, bleeding: then I got scared, after realizing what I had done." These murders—like many others—were a function of male size and strength.

And so it goes; the outcomes of such intense domestic conflicts are not surprising. Sex differences in height and weight are universal; they exist in European, African, and Asian populations as well as in North America. Men are about 10 per cent heavier and 10 per cent taller than women, though these figures vary from one culture to another. The pattern of growth is also relatively constant: boys are slightly taller than girls until girls' adolescent growth spurt begins around age 11 or 12. For about two years girls are taller and heavier than boys; around age 13 or 14 boys' growth spurt begins and the onset of puberty then works to create lifelong sex differences in height and weight.

Men and women also differ markedly in fat distribution and the capacity to undertake and recover from physical work. Studies of large groups of men and women reveal that the male body is approximately 15 per cent fat; in contrast, the female body is about 27 per cent fat. Through intensive training men can reduce their body fat to about 3 per cent; women can reduce body fat to about 12 per cent. If men and women continue to reduce fat beyond these levels through diet, disease, or training, normal physiological functioning is usually impaired—an indication that sex differences in body fat are functional.

Men and women differ dramatically in strength and speed. Women can lift about 65 per cent of what men can lift, carry about 70 per cent of what men can carry, push about 75 per cent of what men can push, and pull about 85 per cent of what men can pull. Studies of handgrip strength suggest that women have about 55 per cent of the grip strength of men. Similarly, the fastest women's times in both short- and long-distance running events are about 15 per cent slower than the fastest men's times.

Men are also better able to put their size, strength, and speed to use. Neuroscientist Charles Rebert studied male and female performance on a video tennis game over a five-day period. Novice male and female subjects scored equally poorly at the outset, but over five days the men's scores increased much more rapidly than the women's scores. Women were more conscientious than men in meeting appointments, more curious about the experiment, and equally interested in obtaining high scores. But they were not as good at playing the game.

Initially, this result is puzzling. There is no obvious reason why a larger, faster, and stronger male should have an advantage in such a contest—learning to press a button quickly in response to a visual stimulus. For Rebert, the results of the study suggest a sex difference in complex visuomotor coordination—men process visuospatial information more quickly and more accurately than women. And this ability makes men a more potent force than women in physical conflict, even when they are similar in size and strength.

Greater size, strength, and speed also increase the likelihood that men will be the victims of male violence. Death from military service is almost exclusively male; more than 99 per cent of the names on the Vietnam Veterans Memorial in Washington, D.C., are male; a full 100 per cent of Americans missing in action in Southeast Asia are men. And, not surprisingly, 94 per cent of prisoners are male. Differences in size, strength, and speed are critical to understanding these figures. Men are more likely to be in jail to some degree because they are more likely to do harm when physical conflicts occur. And men have been sent into war after war at least in part because they are bigger, stronger, and faster than women.

Although differences between men and women in size, strength, and speed may make male violence more likely than violence by women, it is not the largest, strongest, and fastest of men who are inevitably the most violent. In most human populations the wealthy, who tend to be less violent, are physically larger than the poor. Crime, and especially violent crime, is not concentrated among the strongest and largest of men but among men of limited abilities who tend to be poorly educated, relatively uncivil, intolerant, and disadvantaged.

How Size, Strength, and Speed Affect Violent Crime

In virtually every nation-state men comprise more than 90 per cent of those found guilty of murder. The primary methods used to kill differ, however. In Canada about 30 per cent or more of all homicides are committed with firearms and another 30 per cent or so with knives; a further 20 per cent are the consequence of beatings; and a final 10 per cent are strangulations and suffocations. In the United States a little more than 60 per cent of homicides are committed with firearms, and the remaining deaths come from a mix of knifings, beatings, strangulations, and suffocations; as in Canada, knifings and beatings are more common than strangulations and suffocations.

At first glance size, strength, and speed do not appear to be critical factors in most homicides, especially in the United States. The gun has always been known as an "equalizer," allowing a person who is smaller and less powerful to dominate, though men are much more likely to use firearms in homicides than women. In Canada, for the few women who kill, the preferred method is stabbing; they are twice as likely as male suspects to use a knife in their crimes. And in the United States these ratios remain relatively constant: men are more likely to use a firearm, whereas women are more likely to use a knife.

The most likely reason for this difference is that a gun does not give women the same measure of superiority that it provides for men. Because of marked differences in size, strength, and speed, women cannot be confident that they will be able to use a gun to kill someone. They may quite rightly believe that the weapon is likely to be seized and used against them.

Although men kill both men and women, there is one context in which the victims are much more likely to be women than men: the murder of a spouse or lover. In about 70 per cent of these situations, women are the victims. In other kinds of killings—attacks on friends and acquaintances, stranger homicide, robbery homicide, and contract killing—the victims are overwhelmingly male.

Further, with most killings of women, the event takes place in either her home or the home of the suspect (most often the same place). In these private spheres strangulation emerges as an equally likely alternative to shooting, beating, or stabbing. The strangulation of a female victim is about four times as likely as the strangulation of a male victim. (In Canada, for example, less than 4 per cent of male victims are strangled or suffocated, whereas almost 14 per cent of female victims are strangled or suffocated.)

In this context, the size, strength, and speed of men is clearly relevant to the commission of the crime. It is also clear that beatings and knifings are accomplished more easily by human beings of superior size, strength, and speed. In Canada approximately 75 per cent of killings of women depend, at least to some extent, on the male's physical constitution; in the United States about 50 per cent of these killings depend upon this physical superiority.

When I have asked friends and acquaintances to imagine a world in which differences in size, strength, and speed between men and women were reversed, I have received a range of re-

sponses. Some people believe that a preponderance of male violence would remain the norm. Others suggest that we would see a
criminal class of female offenders, a police force populated by
women, and a correctional industry run by women attempting to
protect society from the predatory conduct of women.

Psychologist Dave Albert of Vancouver's University of British
Columbia has spent most of his career studying the biological
origins of violence. He has concluded that men are inherently
no more aggressive than women and, accordingly, that our best explanations for the gender gap lie in the realm of superior size,
strength, and speed.

If Dave Albert is correct, how are we to understand the exceptional sex ratio in spousal killings in the United States, briefly referred to in chapter 2? This phenomenon can be traced back some
fifty years in Chicago, Detroit, and Philadelphia; in these cities,
within a black underclass, spousal killings by women have always
been at least as common as spousal killings by men, and usually
slightly more so. The first and obvious explanation might be that
the ready availability of guns in the United States allows women to
dispatch their larger, stronger, and faster husbands as easily as husbands can dispatch wives. This is what psychologists Martin Daly
and Margo Wilson refer to as "the old equalizer hypothesis."

But the data do not support this hypothesis. Black women who
kill their husbands in the United States are more likely to use
means other than firearms. For example, in Chicago between 1965
and 1990, there were 844 spousal homicides committed by men
and 862 spousal homicides committed by women. In a little more
than 50 per cent of the homicides committed by men a firearm was

the weapon of choice; in a little more than 50 per cent of the homicides committed by women a weapon other than a firearm was the instrument of choice—typically a knife.

What, then, does explain the exceptional sex ratio in spousal homicides in the black underclass of the United States? It is certainly not race itself. Among blacks who live in Africa or in Canada, men are much more likely to kill their spouses than women are. Being a member of an underclass does not seem to be a factor either. Among Latinos living in the United States in similarly socially and economically disadvantaged situations, men again are much more likely to kill their spouses than women are.

As noted in chapter 2, researchers have suggested answers that are imbedded in the social realm: these kinds of killings take place when "women feel socially empowered to retaliate against male coercion." Black women of the underclass are a part of "matrilineal kinship networks"; in these circumstances women with children are likely to "live nearer to and to have more frequent contact with their own genealogical kin than their husband's." In contrast, Latino women are more patrilineal in their living arrangements and their traditions.

But even these spousal killings by black women differ markedly from spousal killings by black men. Males of all races and cultures perpetrate family massacres; women do not. Men kill after subjecting their partners to years of abuse; women do not. Men plan and execute murder-suicides; women do not.

In sum, the exceptional sex ratio in spousal killings is not as dramatic as it appears to be. Even though women in the black underclass are as likely to kill their spouses as their husbands are, the dynamic of the violence is so markedly different that it is almost absurd to speak of an equivalence—to suggest that the actions of these women hold a mirror to the actions of their husbands. Something more than size, strength, and speed continues to divide male violence from the violence of women.

Mathematical and Verbal Abilities

From 1972 to 1979, Camilla Benbow and her doctoral supervisor, Julian Stanley, surveyed Scholastic Aptitude Tests of 10,000 of America's most mathematically gifted grade seven and eight students—5,700 boys and 4,300 girls. They found that over the years boys had consistently outscored girls in mathematical aptitude. Moreover, when the two researchers looked at scores of over 500, boys outnumbered girls by more than 2 to 1; for scores over 600, boys outnumbered girls by 4 to 1; and for scores over 700—the realm of the innately talented—boys outnumbered girls by 13 to 1.

The researchers considered possible explanations for these differences. Earlier studies of high school seniors had been criticized because boys had taken more math classes than girls, but this criticism could not be made of Benbow and Stanley's survey. These grade seven and eight students had all taken an equal number of math courses. Similarly, the claim that these girls had been culturally discouraged from an interest in mathematics seemed improbable. They were, after all, much more talented than most boys at mathematics (falling into the top 2 to 5 per cent of all students on tests of achievement), and when asked by Benbow and Stanley, they reported an interest in mathematics that was no different from the extent of interest expressed by mathematically precocious boys.

On December 5, 1980, Benbow and Stanley published the results of their study in *Science*. They closed their article with the
following paragraph, unaware that their words would unleash an
avalanche of criticism:

> We favor the hypothesis that sex differences in achievement in
> and attitude toward mathematics result from superior male
> mathematical ability, which may in turn be related to greater
> male ability in spatial tasks. This male superiority is probably an
> expression of a combination of both endogenous and exogenous
> variables. We recognize, however, that our data are consistent
> with numerous alternative hypotheses. Nonetheless, the hy-
> pothesis of differential course-taking was not supported. It also
> seems likely that putting one's faith in boy-versus-girl socializa-
> tion processes as the only permissible explanation of the sex
> difference in mathematics is premature.

As a result of this rather tentative conclusion, Benbow and her
mentor were vilified by many within and outside the academic
community. The journal *Science* gave two female mathematicians
an opportunity to respond in the volume following the Benbow article; these two authors argued that "environmental and cultural
factors have not been ruled out"—a point that Benbow and Stanley
had already made in suggesting that their results were "a combination of endogenous and exogenous variables." Another self-
described feminist academic was less cautious in her criticism,
telling *Newsweek*, "If your mother hates math and your father tells
you not to worry your pretty little head about it, do you think that

a math test would be an accurate measurement of your ability?" A Canadian biologist threw a little more gasoline on the fire, telling Canada's *Globe and Mail* that "what we have here are people who are looking for a justification of their own political beliefs."

But Benbow and Stanley were not saying that socialization should be discounted as a factor in shaping mathematical abilities, that girls should be discouraged from embarking upon careers in mathematics, or that males were in any significant sense superior to females. Most important, they were not saying that biology was destiny. After all, the pool of human beings that was the focus of their research—mathematically precocious youth—contained almost as many girls as boys. These 4,300 girls were already more accomplished in mathematics than 95 per cent of their male classmates.

But the researchers were clearly puzzled by the empirical fact that as scores increased, the percentage of boys relative to girls also increased, independent of the extent of formal training and the extent to which mathematics was perceived by these boys and girls to be either an enjoyable or relevant pursuit. Benbow and Stanley said that arguing for socialization as "the only permissible explanation of the sex difference" was "premature."

In political terms, even this cautious conclusion was a mistake. Our culture places great value on mathematical and verbal abilities, the two main components of what we call intelligence. And the suggestion that males might be innately superior in even one small part of intelligence provoked attack. Biologist Anne Fausto-Sterling took Benbow and Stanley to task in her book *Myths of Gender*. In a chapter titled "Are Men Really Smarter than Women?" Fausto-Sterling suggested that any discussion of "natural" causes for a sex difference in mathematical abilities is premature. Fausto-Sterling insisted that only after our society has reformed mathematics education and career counselling could we even begin to think about innate sex differences.

But sex differences that are to some extent innate seem almost a certainty. The Benbow and Stanley research, though pivotal in the debate on the issue, is only part of the evidence supporting the idea that biology plays a role in mathematical ability. Mathematical ability is derived from a compilation of scores on a variety of tests (the mental rotations test, the cards rotation test, the rod-and-frame test, arithmetic and algebra problems, the embedded figures test).

One of these tests—the mental rotations test—produces the most significant sex differences across all cultures. Subjects are asked to look at the images of two or more objects, drawn to represent different views of the three-dimensional form. They are asked to determine which of the objects are similar, a question that requires "mental rotation" of the drawings in front of them. A 1995 review of more than three hundred studies of sex differences in spatial ability, published in *Psychological Bulletin,* found a marked male superiority in the mental rotations test across a wide range of populations. The size of the statistical effect suggests that in a hypothetical group of 100 people, the top 10 on the mental rotations test would include 8 men and 2 women; in the top 50 scores, there would be 33 men and 17 women.

But once again biology does not imply male superiority in any given instance. My wife would almost certainly be one of the 2 women in the top 10 per cent of test scores for a hypothetical group of 100 people; I am confident that I am not one of the men in the top 10 per cent. I turn to my wife for instruction and advice about carpentry, especially when framing a structure, for experience has taught me that in dealing with three dimensions, I do better to trust her instincts than my own.

Some of the most striking evidence in favour of a biological basis for such sex differences comes from the work of Doreen Kimura, a neuropsychologist at the University of Western Ontario. Since 1974 Kimura has been collecting data on brain-damaged men and women. She has found that the brains of men and women react very differently to strokes, tumours, and injuries. Specifically, controls over motion and language appear to be located and organized differently in different parts of the male and female brain.

After damage to the left hemisphere of the brain, both men and women typically suffer losses in motor control. But damage to the front part of the left hemisphere is much more debilitating for women than for men; women are about ten times as likely to have difficulty in arm or hand movements if their injury is in this area. Male motor abilities are usually not affected by a stroke in the front part of the left hemisphere; it appears that in males, control over motor abilities is spread across the entirety of that side of the brain, with concentration in the rear of the hemisphere.

Language also appears to be controlled in different parts of the brain in men and women. About 70 per cent of women who have strokes originating in the anterior region of the left hemisphere of the brain have some language loss, whereas damage to the rest of the hemisphere scarcely affects their language ability. In contrast, men are likely to suffer language loss if the stroke hits any of the regions of the left hemisphere; they are especially vulnerable to a stroke in the parietal region.

Kimura concludes that men and women have very different talents as a result of the dissimilar structure and function of their brains. She also suggests that men predominate in fields such as mathematics and physics, not because women are oppressed or discouraged from participating in these areas, but because their abilities and interests are different from men's.

Although it is scientifically sound to say that the aptitudes of men and women are biologically mediated, some people believe that this statement is a pretext for the domination of women. There is an understandable concern that research such as Kimura's study of brain asymmetry and Benbow and Stanley's analysis of mathematical abilities might cause women to be seen as less "intelligent" than men and be used to justify a policy advantageous to men.

Tests of "intelligence" are, however, not impartial surveys of human abilities. The 1937 revision of the Stanford-Binet test was designed to ensure equal treatment of men and women; items that produced higher male or female scores were eliminated. Similarly, during the 1960s, after several years of higher scores for women, questions that favoured women were deleted. The manipulation of the test continued through the 1980s and '90s, though not to ensure equality between the sexes. The test's designers added more items referring to science, business, and "practical affairs" and reduced the number of items referring to human relations, arts, and humanities.

Men have been the beneficiaries of this change; they can now claim a slight advantage over women in measured aptitude. But this advantage is meaningless: it depends entirely on what is being measured, and as has been seen over time, the selection of items for intelligence tests is not a scientific but a political exercise.

The French psychologist Alfred Binet, the originator of the intelligence test, knew that he was not developing a test of aptitude. His aim was more modest: to develop an empirical test of achievement that would allow schools to identify mentally handicapped and learning-disabled children so that their skills might be improved.

In the last fifty years Binet's intentions have been perverted; his test has been used not to identify weakness but primarily to rank-order the abilities of individuals. As Stephen Jay Gould reminds us, what we call intelligence is a fabrication of our collective imagination. These scores "do not define anything innate or permanent. We may not designate what they measure as intelligence or any other reified entity."

Nevertheless, the studies of Kimura, Benbow and Stanley, and others show that men are more likely to be oriented to physical and spatial realms than women are, at least at the extremes of the population distribution. As a result, men are more likely to look for solutions to difficulties and contradictions by physically manipulating their environments. At first glance this may be a difficult conclusion to accept. If we compare a group of 100 men with a group of 100 women, the differences in spatial and physical skills, especially in the mid-range of the distribution, are not significant; there is a good deal of gender overlap in these areas. But differences between men and women are very significant at the extremes of the population distribution—this is what the research conducted by Benbow and Stanley, Kimura, and others establishes. And violence, understood as a physical imposition upon others, is an extreme behaviour.

Women and the Power of Conversation, Verbal Compromise, and Empathy

In the realm of language, women have an apparent biological advantage, and men have an apparent biological disadvantage. The most widely cited work on sex differences in verbal ability is E. E. Maccoby and C. N. Jacklin's 1974 text, *The Psychology of Sex Differences.* In this book the two psychologists set out what has become the dominant view of a female superiority in verbal abilities. From preschool to early adolescence, boys and girls have similar verbal abilities. Around puberty, the sexes begin to diverge, and female superiority increases through high school and beyond. Girls are better able to speak and to understand what others are saying; they also perform better on both "high-level" verbal tasks (analogies, comprehension of difficult written material, and creative writing) as well as on lower-level measures of verbal ability (fluency).

In the years since the text was published, there have been many challenges to this conventional wisdom—and not all of what Maccoby and Jacklin argued can now be seen as correct. Like mathematical abilities, verbal skills have many constituent parts. Although women excel in a number of these areas, the original claim that women are superior to men on tests of verbal analogies has not been supported by subsequent studies.

A test of verbal analogies depends more on logic and abstract reasoning than on a facility with words. A typical verbal analogies question might set out the word pair "horse: gallop" and then ask which one of the following four sets of words, or analogies, fits best with the initial word pair:

dog: bone
human: run
cow: chew
cat: claw

With this kind of test men are likely to do at least as well as or better than women, recognizing, through a process of abstract reasoning, that "human: run" is most closely analogous to "horse: gallop."

But researchers have found marked female superiority on tests of "associational fluency" or "quality of verbal production," in which subjects are asked to produce synonyms of words such as "dark," "wild," or "strong," or to speak in sentences in response to specific questions. Differences in fluency are often apparent even in toddlers. For example, in one study of sentence construction conducted at the University of Michigan, 2- to 4-year-old girls produced longer sentences than a comparable group of 2- to 4-year-old boys; the girls also made many fewer grammatical errors.

But some researchers have argued (as with male mathematical abilities) that when all of the existing literature is thoroughly canvassed, there is no clear female advantage in verbal ability. Psychologists Janet Shibley Hyde of the University of Wisconsin, Madison, and Marcia Linn of the University of California, Berkeley, have produced the most comprehensive review of gender differences. Using the technique of meta-analysis, an approach that allows a researcher to focus on the outcomes and methodologies of a wide range of studies that all have a similar subject of inquiry, Hyde and Linn looked at the results of 165 studies of male and female verbal abilities. Their conclusion was:

> There are no gender differences in verbal ability, at least at this time, in American culture. A gender difference of one tenth of a standard deviation is scarcely one that deserves continued attention in theory, research, or textbooks. Surely we have larger effects to pursue.

But the apparently small difference that Hyde and Linn identified flows from the very wide range of abilities that they canvassed. Their concluding remarks do not adequately separate the various tests that contribute to the concept that we call verbal ability— instead they have lumped together the abstract reasoning skills that underlie tests of analogy with the associational fluency skills demanded of speech itself. As the authors concede at one point in their article, men talk more than women, but when they looked specifically at tests of the quality of verbal production, there was a distinct female advantage.

It will come as no surprise to many women that men spend more time talking than women, the marginally inferior quality of our speech aside. Again, a more general point is that biology is not destiny. To place the results in concrete terms: in a group of 100 people, the top 50 in quality of speech would include 30 females and 20 males. This is a significant difference but far from an un-equivocally clear relationship between biology and a specific type of verbal ability. In addition, the difference observed does not suggest that any given boy or man will necessarily produce speech that is inferior to that of any given girl or woman.

The way that men and women talk to each other has been analyzed by psycholinguist Deborah Tannen, author of the popular book *You Just Don't Understand.* In her more academically oriented book *Gender and Discourse,* Tannen discussed an often cited finding from a range of research studies: men interrupt women far more often than women interrupt men. Two researchers recorded naturally occurring conversations on campus locations. They reported that 96 per cent of the interruptions they observed were initiated by men. A study of 40 preschool children found that males interrupted conversation twice as often as females. Many young boys find cooperation difficult and cannot keep up with young girls. In response, they resort to interruption and annoyed silence to establish control and avoid their biologically mediated inadequacies.

But it is at the lowest point on the scale of verbal abilities that the differences between men and women become most salient. Stutterers and severe dyslexics are three or four times as likely to be male as female. As Robert Pool has noted in his exhaustive study of sex differences, it's difficult to think of a good explanation for these very striking ratios—found across cultures—that doesn't include male biology as a relevant variable. The inability to communicate produces profound frustration, and at the social margins of our culture such difficulties can lead to a disproportionate amount of male aggression and violence.

It is also likely that women are more empathetic than men, again for reasons that have some origin in biology. There have been a number of research reports that measure empathy in different ways—through the facial expressions of four- to six-year-old girls and boys, through verbal reports of the feelings of similarly aged boys and girls, and through the cries of newborn babies responding to the taped sound of another infant's cry. In all of these reports, with newborns and preschool children, females display more empathy than males. Martin Hoffman of the University of Michigan, writing in *Psychological Bulletin,* concludes of this research that there is likely a "constitutional precursor" that when linked to socialization can account for longstanding adult sex differences in empathy.

Differences in Sexuality

Male anatomy is an important precursor to male violence. The penis and the requirement of erection before sexual intercourse have no analogy in female anatomy. For a woman to "force" a man to engage in sexual relations, she must ensure that he is erect and willing and able to participate. The erect male needs no such cooperation from the female; the anatomically receptive vagina can be forced to accommodate an erect penis.

The feminist author Susan Brownmiller has argued that as a consequence of these anatomical differences, every man is a potential rapist and the act of sex is "nothing more than a conscious process of intimidation by which all men keep all women in a state of fear." Brownmiller suggests that rape is best described as a political crime, the male's ultimate technique for keeping the female subordinated as the second sex.

There is probably some merit in Brownmiller's argument. Although her description of every male's intent—"a conscious process of intimidation"—is exaggerated and even demeaning, the anatomical differences between men and women do give some legitimacy to the notion that every man is a potential rapist. And these anatomical differences go a long way towards explaining why sexual assaults with violence are almost exclusively the province of the male. Nevertheless, in contemporary North America only a very small percentage of men commit violent sexual attacks; cultural forces (opposition from both men and women) limit both opportunities and interest in sexual violence. But in societies with fewer constraints on the use of male force, rape is a relatively common occurrence. In contemporary South Africa, for example, it is estimated that one in three women will be raped by the time she enters her twenties. Similarly, in times of war, when virtually all social rules have been discarded, rape is commonplace. The Bosnian rape camps have parallels in every era of human history. When the thin veneer of civilization and the rule of law are removed, historical experience dictates that many men will force sex on unwilling women.

A more difficult question, beyond the obvious distinctions of anatomy, is whether males and females are fundamentally different in their sexual inclinations and desires. The anatomical differences between men and women clearly give rise to different capabilities; the penis can be used as a weapon in a manner that the vagina cannot. But are our approaches to sexuality also fundamentally different, thus influencing the manner in which we relate and hence the potential for male violence? Are we sexually aroused by different stimuli, for different reasons, and in different contexts?

Before the development of an oral contraceptive, every act of sexual intercourse carried the risk of pregnancy for women. Sexual intercourse outside marriage was a physical and social minefield, except for those in roles of mistress or prostitute. The production of "bastard" children brought shame and, in many instances, isolation from the community and one's family. The birth control pill changed all of this.

Studies in England, Canada, and the United States have charted these changes. From the 1960s to the present, women have had intercourse at a much younger age. Women born in 1920 had their first sex at the age of 20, almost always in the context of marriage. Women born in 1970 had their first sexual intercourse at the age of 17, almost always out of wedlock.

But there remain differences in how men and women approach sexuality. Research indicates that men, regardless of their date of birth, tend to have many more sex partners in a lifetime than do women. While one-third of all males in North America have had more than ten sexual partners, slightly less than 10 per cent of women have had a similar number.

And men and women tend to have different preferences. Whereas less than 10 per cent of women in America between the ages of 18 and 44 find group sex "very" or "somewhat appealing," almost five times as many men in the same age bracket find this kind of coupling to their liking. Similarly, whereas only 10 per cent of women find sex with a stranger appealing, more than three times as many men like the idea. And whereas 54 per cent of adult males report that they think about sex every day or several times a day, only 19 per cent of women say they think about sex that frequently.

These sorts of sex differences are more easily seen in the consumption of pornography—magazines, videos, and strip shows. The audience for this material is and has always been largely male; male consumption of pornography has never had much of a female equivalent. And yet the autosexuality that is at the heart of pornography would seem to have a greater adaptive or functional value for women than for men. The consequences of sexuality are, after all, so much more profound for women. All other things being equal, one might think that women would be more drawn to pornography than men, since it permits a sexual arousal without consequence, the ability to obtain sexual pleasure without the risk of pregnancy.

In the 1970s, psychologists Russell Knoth and Kelly Boyd surveyed almost 400 boys and girls aged 12 to 18, asking them about their first sexual arousal. The boys reported first sexual arousal near the start of puberty, usually in response to a visual stimulus. Girls reported first sexual arousal two to three years after puberty, typically in a social and romantic context. More dramatically, boys reported that sexual arousal occurred several times daily; girls reported sexual arousal once or twice a week. Boys, in contrast to girls, also reported that these instances of sexual arousal were very intense and very distracting. The authors later replicated these findings with 262 students aged 17 to 54 years, based at East Coast universities in the United States. The results were similar; women's arousal was significantly more dependent on being in a relationship than men's arousal was.

And yet physiologically, women are as aroused by sexual material as men are. Although women are not inclined to seek out pornographic images, they do become aroused when these images are placed in front of them. Americans Hillel Rubinsky and David Eckerman measured the genital response of male and female subjects between the ages of 21 and 39 first as they watched sexually neutral films and then as they watched erotic films. Both sexes showed moderate to large increases in genital response during the erotic films. Similarly, in the Netherlands, researchers tested women's physiological responses to erotic films made by men and erotic films made by women. The researchers recorded vaginal pulse amplitude continuously during both types of presentations; they found that genital arousal during both types of films was substantial.

While men and women do not appear to differ significantly in their physiological response to explicit sexual images, adolescent boys and girls and adult men and women report that different kinds of stimuli propel sexual interest. Men are aroused by nudity, and the more explicit the nudity, the greater the arousal; women, in contrast, are more likely to be aroused by the emotional and social context of an encounter. Further, from puberty onward men focus on sexual thoughts and imagery much more than women do. Young men also appear to be more distracted and consumed by sexual desire than young women.

Those in favour of a cultural explanation for these differences in sexual arousal blame the pornography industry, which encourages men to think of women as sexual objects, a visually stimulating collage of breasts, buttocks, and vaginas. But men, regardless of their exposure to pornography, are at a very young age more likely to think about and focus on sex than women are and to be physically aroused by visual stimuli.

Male and female sexual arousal have different biological origins; the leering male, so pilloried in some feminist accounts of sexuality, has a biological predisposition to focus on anonymous lips, breasts, thighs, and buttocks. And when this responsiveness to visual stimuli is linked with a conception of the penis as a weapon, it is clear that male sexuality predisposes men to violence in a way that female sexuality does not. Warren Farrell captures this sex difference in an anecdote from his book *The Myth of Male Power*:

> A pinup at work symbolizes to many women that the man cares more about a woman's body than about a woman's work. The woman who is serious about work feels she has to deal with a man who wants to combine the two—without regard for her desire.
>
> Many women respond to pinups of women by bringing in pinups of men: "This'll show 'em." But it has the opposite effect. It signals to men that the woman is so interested in men's bodies and sex that she can't stop thinking of it while she's working. Which is fine with him.

This observed difference has its roots in biology. The male focus on visual stimuli for sexual arousal translates into a greater tendency to objectify women. Men separate the body from the person more easily than women do, and this objectification, coupled with the penis as weapon, makes sexual violence more likely for men than for women. Fortunately, culture and socialization are powerful constraints on male sexual violence in most Western industrial cultures. But male anatomy and male sexual response, along with the prevalence of rape in places such as contemporary South Africa and Bosnia and in the global experiences of every century, are powerful testimony to Susan Brownmiller's important caution that every man is a potential rapist.

A Final Caveat

The Israeli kibbutz demonstrates how gender equality can coexist with acceptance of significant sex differences. The kibbutz was inspired by Marxist idealism of the 1920s and was devoted to common ownership of property and equality of gender. These values remain, for the most part, today. The kibbutz has shed private property, places an equal value on all forms of work, and is the backbone of an agriculturally based rural economy.

But in its first fifty years, the kibbutz has not eliminated sex differences in job preferences, political activity, and child rearing. Although every member of the kibbutz receives the same wage for work, men outnumber women by more than 10 to 1 in plumbing and electrical work, 7 to 1 in agriculture, and 2 to 1 in industry and management roles. Conversely, women outnumber men by a ratio of more than 6 to 1 in service jobs and more than 9 to 1 in preschool and elementary teaching. Robert Pool has concluded that the kibbutz experience has important implications for the study of sex differences.

> Two lessons emerge from the kibbutz experience. First, it is exceptionally difficult to form a society that has sexual equality in its identity version, with men and women doing exactly the same things. The ideological, highly committed kibbutzniks

succeeded in replacing capitalism with communism, they succeeded in transforming an urban, paternalistic society into a
rural, sexually democratic one, but they failed to abolish the
sexual divisions of labor and the mother-child bond.

But second, it doesn't really matter. The kibbutzniks decided that sexual identity wasn't necessary for sexual equality
after all. In their world, men and women are equal in the ways
that matter, even if they don't do exactly the same things.

So men and women often make quite divergent choices about
their occupations, in large measure because male and female
brains are wired differently. Understanding this difference is a first
step towards recognizing that boys and men are more violent than
girls and women for reasons that we cannot lay at the altar of
socialization. Every culture has a preponderance of men who have
superior spatial and physical abilities; who are larger, stronger,
and faster; and who are more ready, willing, and able to physically
manipulate their environments. And every culture has a preponderance of women with superior verbal fluency and empathy
who can talk through, soothe, and resolve social disputes. Male
anatomy and sexuality are also critical to the genesis of male violence; only men commit rape because only men are biologically
equipped to do so. This amalgam of differences, taken as a whole,
is critical to solving the puzzle of why men are the violent sex.

Chapter Four

Bred in the Bone

What's bred in the bone will come out in the flesh.

PROVERB

On May 21, 1998, 15-year-old Kip Kinkel arrived at Thurston High School in Springfield, Oregon, armed with a semiautomatic Ruger rifle, two handguns, and a knife. He opened fire with the rifle in the school's cafeteria, spraying bullets in every direction; two students were killed and seventeen injured. Before coming to school he had shot and killed his parents in the family home, and as the police were arresting him he managed to stab an officer before finally being taken into custody.

For years before that day Kip had displayed bizarre and violent behaviour, even though he grew up in an upper-middle-class home with two apparently caring parents. He boasted about stuffing firecrackers into a cat's mouth and down gopher holes; he was arrested by police for throwing rocks at cars from an overpass; and he was suspended from school on many occasions for misbehaviour, once for karate-kicking another student in the head.

He had some difficulty with learning in school and an obsession with violence. He excitedly told one of his friends that he wanted to place a bomb under the school's bleachers during a pep rally and then block the doorway so that the students couldn't get out. He built five bombs on the basis of material found on the Internet, and he wrote in his journal about his plans "to kill everybody." His parents tried many different treatments, including Ritalin, Prozac, and psychiatric counselling. They also provided him with summer trips to Spain and Costa Rica; tennis, sailing, and skiing lessons; martial arts training; and the Ruger rifle and the two handguns that he used to kill them.

In hindsight, there were plenty of signs that Kip Kinkel was a very disturbed young man, but as Jonathan Kellerman has pointed out, Bill and Faith Kinkel rewarded their very dangerous son for his difficulties with a collection of lethal weapons. "Was there some need to keep Kip bad?" Kellerman asks "Or had these poor parents simply been beaten down by years of threats and rage and finally relented out of fear of what Kip might do if they continued to frustrate his lust for guns?"

We cannot know what might have saved Kip Kinkel from his murderous rampage (giving him firearms was obviously not a good idea), but we do know that he possessed personality attributes, independent of his environment, that placed him at great risk of doing harm. He had always been a sadistic child who was cruel to animals, had behavioural difficulties in school, and was obsessed with violence and weapons.

Could anyone have predicted his murderous spree? Researchers have established that certain characteristics increase the probability that an individual will be violent: being male, having a previous history of violence or threatening violence, doing poorly in
school, having learning difficulties, and being suspended or expelled from school. Kip Kinkel possessed all of these attributes.

Lombroso's Criminal Man

Kip Kinkel seems to have been predisposed to violence in a way
that most men are not. The idea that some men are violent by their
very nature has been around in science for at least one hundred
years, and there are many less direct references in literature to this
phenomenon during the past two thousand years. Cesare Lombroso, an Italian psychiatrist who lived in Europe during the latter
half of the 19th century, developed the first scientific theory of "the
criminal man."

Lombroso believed that such men were compelled towards a
life of crime and even formed a distinct species, *Homo delinquens*,
as a result of congenital weaknesses. He also believed that this
born criminal was an atavistic being, a throwback to an earlier era,
or as he put it, "the relic of a vanished race." In other words, born
criminals were like primitive peoples or children. Finally, Lombroso contended that a criminal type could be identified, and his
behaviour predicted, largely on the basis of cranial, facial, and
body measurements.

Lombroso's ideas about a criminal type applied to men only. He
saw prostitution as the equivalent of male criminality, and in those
rare circumstances in which women committed crimes outside of

prostitution, Lombroso said these were "the feminine equivalent of criminality in the male, because they satisfy the desire for licence, idleness and indecency, characteristic of the criminal nature."

Lombroso began to think about the problem of criminals when he was a doctor serving in the Italian army in the mid-1860s. He initially thought that what separated "the honest soldier from his vicious comrade" were tattoos: "the indecency of the designs that covered his body." But as he later said, the idea that these designs could separate criminals from noncriminals "bore no fruit."

Then, after an especially notorious criminal died in jail, Lombroso was called on to conduct the postmortem. What he saw when he cut open the man's skull was, in his words,

> not merely an idea, but a revelation. At the sight of that skull, I seemed to see all of a sudden, lighted up as a vast plain under a flaming sky, the problem of the nature of the criminal—an atavistic being who reproduces in his person the ferocious instincts of primitive humanity and the inferior animals. Thus were explained anatomically the enormous jaws, high cheek bones, prominent superciliary arches, solitary line in the palms, extreme size of the orbits, handle-shaped or sessile ears found in criminals, savages, and apes, insensibility to pain, extremely acute sight, tattooing, excessive idleness, love of orgies, and the irresistible craving for evil for its own sake, the desire not only to extinguish life in the victim, but to mutilate the corpse, tear its flesh, and drink its blood.

When Lombroso's ideas, based upon his observations of a few skulls and their social history, were actually tested in Britain in the early 20th century, no empirical support emerged for "criminal man" and his odd blend of tattoos, idleness, sexual mania, and handle-shaped ears. In his often cited work, *The English Convict,* Charles Goring compared three thousand convicted criminals with hospital patients, college students, and soldiers. The criminals weighed less, were shorter, and had lower verbal and mathematical intelligence scores than the other groups, but no evidence could be found of Lombroso's "anthropological monster" lurking in their midst.

William Sheldon and Somatotyping

Lombroso's failure to establish physique as a predictor of male criminality did not dissuade others from following his line of argument, albeit with modifications. American William Sheldon was the father of somatotyping, a method of classifying the personalities of individuals on the basis of body type. Sheldon identified three body types—ectomorphs, mesomorphs, and endomorphs—and in the 1940s and 1950s argued that every human being could be classified on an ectomorph-mesomorph-endomorph scale; this scale was said to reflect not only differences in body size and shape but also differences in mood and temperament. Ectomorphs were predominantly thin and introverted; mesomorphs, predominantly muscular, extroverted, and aggressive; and endomorphs, predominantly soft, limp, and easygoing. Sheldon ranked individuals on a seven-point scale for each of the three types: ectomorph, mesomorph, and endomorph. A person with a 2-5-2 ranking, for example, was said to be predominantly mesomorphic.

Sheldon argued that mesomorphs were overrepresented among delinquents and that skilful somatotyping could identify young men at risk for future crime. In 1939 he was appointed the clinical director of the Massachusetts Hayden Goodwill Inn, a home for boys in conflict with the law. Sheldon asked the boys to strip naked and took photographs from the back, side, and front to construct individual somatotypes; he also wrote detailed biographies for each boy to link social history to the somatotype.

Sheldon's work on the relationship between physique and temperament became very popular in the United States: *Life* magazine ran a cover story in 1951 setting out his theory of somatotypes (even today the ecto-meso-endo trilogy continues in popular culture). Sheldon and his colleagues even tried to relate the size of male and female genitalia to temperament. According to Sheldon, a masculine temperament flows from a large penis and testes in the male and from small breasts, coupled with a large clitoris and labia, in the female. Unfortunately for Sheldon, there is no evidence to suggest that the size of male (or female) genitalia can predict male temperament, or more specifically, male aggression.

But there is a limited connection between a person's physique and personality, and research continues today in this area. *Psychological Abstracts* lists more than one hundred academic articles on somatotypes and behaviour published in journals between 1981 and 1996. In one 1993 study in the *Journal of Forensic Sciences* the authors compared the somatotypes of rapists with those of pedophiles, finding that rapists were somewhat more muscular and had less body fat than pedophiles; the authors noted that the extent of the physical differences between the two groups was not terribly significant.

The xyy Man

In the 1960s research into the linkage between violent crime and biology became more sophisticated, drawing upon the burgeoning discipline of genetics. Researcher Patricia Jacobs reported that a disproportionately large percentage of violent men in Scottish prisons had an extra y chromosome—a genetic anomaly that affects about one in a thousand men in the general population. Women typically inherit two x chromosomes and men an x and a y chromosome; in these exceptional cases men receive two y chromosomes. Jacobs and her colleagues, in their survey of several Scottish jails, found ten to twenty times as many men with the extra y chromosome as would have been anticipated. They described these xyy chromosome males as "double" males or "super" males and suggested that such men were taller than average and more inclined to criminal behaviour.

But subsequent studies of prison inmates and re-interpretation of Jacobs's data have failed to support this finding. There is consistent evidence that xyy chromosome males are more likely to be tall and to have poor intelligence test scores, but there is no consistent finding that they are overrepresented in the prison population. Perhaps most telling, approximately 98 per cent of xyy males are never institutionalized for criminal behaviour.

These findings do not mean, however, that the xyy chromosome is completely unrelated to crime, only that the relationship is not overwhelming or especially compelling for diagnostic purposes; the xyy male is rarely a dangerous predator. A Danish study published in 1976 selected the tallest 15 per cent of Danish men born between 1944 and 1947—a total of more than 4,000 men. The researchers selected this pool of subjects knowing that all XYY males could be found within this grouping of 4,000. As anticipated, given the height restriction, there was a greater representation of XYY men than within the general population—a total of 12. And 5 of the 12—a little more than 40 per cent—had been convicted of crime. In contrast, the conviction rate among the remaining XY males in the sample was 9 per cent.

This study suggests that there is some correlation between XYY and the tendency to crime: 40 per cent of the XYY men had criminal records, in contrast to less than 10 per cent of the XY men. But because 98 per cent of the XYY men were never sent to jail for their crimes and 60 per cent were never convicted of any criminal offence, the value of the XYY chromosome as a diagnostic or predictive tool has to be seen as quite limited. But this conclusion does not mean that there is no connection at all.

Studies of Twins and Adopted Children: A Genetic Link

Long before Patricia Jacobs began her inquiries into the link between XYY males and criminality, other researchers suggested that genetic structure might be related to criminal behaviour. In the 1920s German physician Johannes Lange compared the criminal behaviours of identical and fraternal twins. Lange reasoned that if genetic variables contribute in some way to the likelihood of crime, the criminal records of identical twins should be more similar than the criminal records of fraternal twins.

If environment is the overriding variable, identical twins raised in the same family environment should have criminal records that are similar to the criminal records of fraternal twins raised in the same family environment. Although it could be argued that parents might treat identical twins more similarly than they would fraternal twins, it seems unlikely that this distinction would hold true across all families. Thus, if the criminal records of identical twins were more similar than those of fraternal twins, genetic structure would appear to be the overriding variable.

Lange located 30 pairs of twins, making sure that at least 1 of each pair had a criminal conviction. He found that in 10 of 13 pairs of identical twins both had criminal histories, whereas in only 2 of 17 pairs of fraternal twins did both have a criminal record. From the 1920s to the present a host of other researchers have replicated Lange's findings, using much larger sample sizes in a range of countries, including the Netherlands, Finland, the United States, Japan, Denmark, and Norway. A consistent pattern has emerged: identical twins are about twice as likely as fraternal twins to share a criminal history.

Moreover, in one American study in which twins were asked about the extent to which they shared activities, those who reported more shared activities were no more similar to each other in criminal history than those who reported few shared activities. This is a major finding, and one that has not been given enough weight or thought in the study of criminal behaviour.

Genetics appears to be a more potent predictor of criminal behaviour than environment, at least in the context of identical twins. Additionally, the lowest rate of similarity in criminal history appears with fraternal twins of different sexes, repeating the common finding that women are much less likely than men to commit crimes.

Researchers have also looked at the criminal records of adopted children to determine whether the criminal history of biological parents or of adoptive parents has a greater influence on the behaviour of adopted children. The most comprehensive study of adopted children and crime was undertaken in Denmark and published in *Science* in 1984. Sarnoff Mednick and his colleagues based their findings on a sample of more than 14,400 male and female adoptees—the total of all nonfamilial adoptions in Denmark between 1924 and 1947. The researchers looked to see whether either of the biological parents or the adoptive parents had a criminal record and then correlated these findings with the criminal records of the adoptive children.

They found that if neither the biological nor the adoptive parents had a criminal conviction, a little more than 13 per cent of the adopted boys had at least one conviction. That percentage rose slightly, to almost 15 per cent, if an adoptive parent but not a biological parent had a criminal record. If a biological parent but not an adoptive parent had a criminal record, 20 per cent of the adopted boys had at least one criminal conviction. And in those instances where both an adoptive and a biological parent had criminal records, almost 25 per cent of the boys had at least one criminal conviction. What emerged quite clearly, and at the level of statistical significance, was the conclusion that the criminality of the biological parents is more strongly correlated with crime in adopted children than is the criminality of adoptive parents.

The finding is completely at odds with the wisdom of popular culture. We tend to—or want to—believe that environment is the critical factor in producing crime. But this very thorough research

covering more than fourteen thousand adoptees suggests the opposite: that biology is more critical than environment in shaping
behaviour. Simply put, there is a genetic basis for predisposition
to crime.

To be fair, one must acknowledge that even in those instances
where both biological and adoptive parents had criminal records,
more than 75 per cent of the boys did not become involved in
crime, or at the least were not convicted of any criminal offences.
One additional finding from the Mednick study does deserve mention, however. The researchers found that the more substantial the
criminal record of the biological parents, the greater the likelihood
that a son adopted by someone else would have a criminal record.
A biological parent with three or more convictions was three times
as likely to produce an adopted son with a criminal conviction than
a biological parent without any criminal convictions; this relationship did not hold for adoptive parents.

Similar research has been carried out in Sweden. The Stockholm Adoption Study has established that a male adoptee's biological parents exert a greater influence on future crime than do his
adoptive parents. Michael Bohman looked at 862 men and 913
women born between 1930 and 1950 and adopted at an early age
into families with "a relatively good and stable socio-economic stan-
dard." Bohman's findings were very similar to those of Mednick and
his colleagues. If predisposition to crime was both genetically low
and environmentally low, less than 3 per cent of these adopted
men were ever convicted of crime. If the postnatal environment was
high risk and the genetic heritage was low risk, the probability of
conviction was a little less than 7 per cent. If, however, genetic her-

itage was high risk and postnatal environment was low risk, a little more than 12 per cent of the adopted men were convicted of crime. Finally, as in the Mednick study, there was a synergistic connection between the more critical factor of genetic background and environment. If both the pre- and postnatal environments were high risk, the probability of conviction for a male adoptee was 40 per cent.

In a recent discussion of adoption cohorts and the role of genetics in crime, Mednick and his colleagues noted that results from adoption studies have consistently revealed a stronger relationship between the criminal behaviour of a biological father and an adopted son than between the criminal behaviour of an adoptive father and an adopted son.

It must be pointed out, however, that all of these studies deal with property crime; there are no studies linking violent crime in biological parents to violent crime in adoptees. The reason for this inability to connect biology definitively to violent crime is to be found in the very low rate of violent crime relative to property crime. For example, in the Stockholm Adoption Study, fewer than 40 of the 862 men had criminal records, and these records were overwhelmingly records of property crime. Put differently, the existence of a criminal record in these adoption cohorts is relatively rare; criminal records for crimes of violence are substantially less likely than criminal records for property crime. At present, for example, the rate of convictions for property crime in the United States and Canada outstrips the rate of convictions for violent crime by a ratio of up to ten to one. Given the size of cohorts in the adoption studies to date, it would be virtually impossible to achieve a relationship of statistical significance between genetic heritage and violent crime. But the finding of a relationship between property crime and biological background is testimony to the strength of the genetic predisposition.

The Heritability of Personality Traits

It is not only with studies of identical twins and adopted children that a link between biology and crime can be made. For almost fifty years psychologists have been using the MMPI—the Minnesota Multiphasic Inventory—to identify psychological difficulties. A subject is asked to respond "true," "false," or "cannot say" to 566 statements, such as "I am usually a happy person," "Everything tastes the same," and "I have never been in conflict with the law."

The test identifies ten conditions or characteristics:

1. Hypochondriasis—abnormal preoccupation with physical complaints.
2. Depression—feelings of hopelessness and self-deprecation.
3. Hysteria—stress avoidance by conversion into physical and mental symptoms.
4. Psychopathic deviance—conflict with authority and shallow personal attachments.
5. Masculinity-femininity—with high scores representing opposite-sex attitudes and behaviours.
6. Paranoia—undue defensiveness, suspiciousness, and sensitivity.
7. Psychoasthenia—feelings of anxiety, indecision, fearfulness, and guilt.

8. Schizophrenia—bizarre thought and affect, and withdrawal from personal contact.

9. Hypomania—unproductive hyperactivity.

10. Social introversion—social insecurity and shyness.

Not surprisingly, criminals have been more likely to show up on the psychopathic deviance scale than noncriminals. Some of the items on this scale specifically ask about criminal convictions. But what would happen if this scale were given to 13- and 14-year-old boys, before they had committed crimes? Could it predict, on the basis of pre-existing personality traits, who would commit crimes and who would not?

In 1947 two researchers at the University of Minnesota gave the MMPI to four thousand boys and girls in Minneapolis public schools before they had any opportunity to commit crimes. They found that boys with high scores on the psychopathic deviance, schizophrenia, and hypomania scales were most likely to become delinquent. They also found that boys with high scores on the depression, masculinity-femininity, and social-introversion scales rarely committed crimes later in life. According to this research, a clustering of certain personality characteristics (partly or largely a function of a person's genes) is correlated with criminal behaviour.

The successor to the MMPI, the CPI or California Psychological Inventory, also describes a constellation of personality traits that make crime more likely. Like the MMPI, the CPI establishes deviation from a population norm. For example, one of its eighteen scales measures "social presence"; another, "socialization." Criminals have been identified as scoring poorly on the socialization scale. As explained by the scale's founder, Harrison Gough of the University of California at Berkeley, criminals are less likely than noncriminals to be concerned about the rights of others and more likely to display impulsive behaviour, to be unable to form lasting attachments to others, to have poor judgement and planning, to project blame onto others, to take no responsibility for failures, and to be emotionally impoverished.

Gough applied the socialization scale to 26,000 individuals, including juvenile and adult offenders and nonoffenders, in ten countries: Austria, Costa Rica, France, Germany, India, Italy, Puerto Rico, South Africa, Switzerland, and the United States. The scale was translated into eight languages. In every country the scale discriminated between offenders and nonoffenders, independent of any correlation with intelligence scores, age, or socioeconomic status. When those variables were controlled, self-described personality traits continued to divide criminals from noncriminals in all ten countries.

We all know people, occasionally ourselves, who demonstrate "poor judgement and planning in attaining defined goals." And when we see a cluster of these traits in a person—"almost complete lack of dependability," "a tendency to project blame onto others," "impulsive," and "meaningless prevarication"—we can often find family members or friends who, if only occasionally, match this description all too neatly. At the same time there is evidence from ten countries that these characteristics, taken in aggregate over thousands of human beings, differentiate criminals from noncriminals. A self-described failure to socialize—a particular kind of personality and temperament—is typically an important precursor of male violence.

Most people would probably be willing to accept the idea that the failure to socialize is an important precursor of male violence. But what about the possibility that certain kinds of personality traits can be inherited? The best available data suggest that some individuals are born with personalities that predispose them to criminal activity.

In the early 1960s John Shields of London's Maudsley Hospital looked for the presence or absence of three specific personality characteristics among samples of identical and fraternal twins, in some instances raised separately and in other instances raised together. The three personality characteristics were intelligence, extroversion, and neuroticism. The intelligent person is verbally and mathematically able and typically more likely to secure resources for himself and his family. The extrovert is best described by adjectives such as assertive, active, outgoing, outspoken, dominant, forceful, adventurous, noisy, and bossy. The neurotic is best described by adjectives such as tense, anxious, nervous, moody, worrying, fearful, self-pitying, despondent, and emotional. Although there is a well-understood and established genetic linkage with intelligence, the notion that extroversion and neuroticism can be passed from one generation to the next is more contentious.

To identify the presence of these characteristics, Shields administered pen-and-paper tests to 44 pairs of identical twins who had been raised together, 44 pairs of identical twins who had been

raised apart, and 28 pairs of fraternal twins who had been raised together. He found that the most similar pairs of twins, especially in
extroversion and neuroticism, were identical twins brought up separately, not identical twins raised in the same home and not fraternal twins raised in the same home. Once again, research evidence
suggests that genetic structure has a greater impact on the construction of personality than the environment in which a person
has been raised.

As the famed British psychologist Hans Eysenck has noted,
there is a strong belief in most Western cultures in what might be
called a technological or "manipulative" outlook on life. We tend to
believe that it is our environment and what we make of ourselves
that is critical to the development of our personalities and ourselves as social beings; we also believe, albeit to a lesser extent,
that our environment gives rise to our abilities and hence to our opportunities for intellectual and physical performance. As a result of
this kind of thinking we tend to argue that crime is inevitably the
consequence of bad parenting, inadequate opportunity, and material and cultural deprivation. But inadequate opportunity and material deprivation are only a part of the portrait of criminal behaviour;
researchers have revealed that genetic structure can be more sta-
tistically significant than environment in determining who will become a criminal.

Research also suggests that a male who has a combination of
intellectual limitations, difficulties in learning, and certain personality characteristics may be predisposed to aggression, although
intellectual limitations and learning disabilities are not, in them-

selves, risk factors for involvement in crime. But when these attributes are linked, and then joined with a difficult personality, a kind of synergism occurs; the risk of involvement in crime markedly increases.

Nature-Nurture Interactions: An Unexplored Frontier

One of the most common questions asked of criminologists is a relatively simple one: which criminal offenders are most likely to repeat their crimes? The study of recidivism is obviously of great importance to parole decision makers, to judges sentencing those convicted of criminal offences, and to our society in general.

After studying large populations of convicted men in the United States, Canada, and Britain, researchers have concluded that the greatest risk of re-offending is to be found in a male under the age of 24 with a previous record of crime, poor school performance, a record of suspension or expulsion from school, and severe learning disabilities who is living in a single-parent family subsisting on social assistance, mixing with delinquents and criminals, and spending most of his leisure time aimlessly. These characteristics are clearly a mix of genetic traits and environmental stressors—a portrait of a young man who is both biologically and environmentally at risk.

The tendency to commit crime at a very young age (typically between the early teens and early twenties) is a cultural constant that flows from male biology. Similarly, learning disabilities and poor school performance are directly linked to an individual's genetic heritage. Being suspended or expelled from school, mixing with delinquents, and spending leisure time aimlessly have both biological and environmental roots. These activities are more likely among boys who have conflicts with authority, shallow personal attachments, unproductive hyperactivity, and bizarre thought and affect. But a poor environment—growing up in a family subsisting on government handouts or being part of a community of delinquents—can also assist in the development of a criminal career.

We must throw away the simplistic idea that there is a useful debate to be had in mulling over the influences of nature and nurture in the creation of violent crime. There is nothing to be gained—and much to be lost—in thinking about this problem as an either-or proposition. Both genes and environment are critical to understanding why some young men are violent and others are not. Progress in responding to the longstanding affliction of male violence will require an integrated approach. We must recognize that young men like Kip Kinkel are not simply products of their environment—that an intensive regimen of structure and assistance will be needed if we are to overcome what has been bred in the bone.

Chapter Five

The Testosterone Connection

*For nothing, according to Beth, makes women more resistant
to venal temptations than the lack of a penis and its attendant fluid
and fluid sacs. Penis owners are more violent, their will more
concentrated—that much is indisputable. . . .
"Don't you think," Beth asks her new husband, "that an
uncontrollable rush of testosterone would impede the sort of moral
deliberation required to, you know, achieve perfect goodness?"
"I'll have to think about that," Larry says.*

CAROL SHIELDS, LARRY'S PARTY

In June of 1889, the then renowned French physician Charles
Edouard Brown Sequard shocked the Paris meeting of the Soci-
eté de biologie by announcing that testicles contain an invigorat-
ing substance that can be extracted from animals and injected into
humans, with astonishing results. Even more amazing to those as-
sembled, Brown Sequard revealed that he had been the subject of
his own study. He had prepared a mixture of blood and seminal

fluid derived from the testicles of healthy dogs and guinea pigs and then, after a thorough filtering, injected the substance ten times during a three-week period.

The results were startling. The 72-year-old scientist told the society that his mental concentration and physical endurance had improved dramatically. He was now able to walk farther without resting and to lift an extra 6 or 7 kilograms of weight; his bowel was more vigorous. For reasons unknown, he also determined that the length of the arc of his urine had increased by 25 per cent.

Once word of Brown Sequard's findings spread, other physicians in Europe and America engaged in similar experiments with elderly men, usually reporting comparable results. Those injected with testicular extracts reported diminished pain, increased sexual interest, and a general improvement in their mental and physical states; a fountain of youth appeared to be on the horizon.

Although Brown Sequard did not speak of aggression as a consequence of his injections, there was considerable hostility to the morality of his experiments. In a letter circulated to British physicians just a month after Brown Sequard's initial announcement, Dr. Edward Berdoe wrote:

> The object of these abominable proceedings is to enable broken down libertines to pursue with renewed vigour the excesses of their youth, to rekindle the dying embers of lust in the debilitated and aged, and to profane the bodies of men which are the temples of God by an elixir drawn from the testicles of dogs and rabbits by a process involving the excruciating torture of the innocent animals, which elixir is then injected by

a physician into the veins of his patient whom he has caused
to practice a degrading and loathsome vice.

Brown Sequard's experiments ran counter to the antivivisec-
tion movement of the day, and his talk of sexual tonics ran contrary
to Victorian morality. Moreover, unscrupulous entrepreneurs began to market "elixirs of life" in an unregulated market, paying little
attention to the risks of injection or the safe preparation of the testicular extract. The result was that Brown Sequard, a distinguished
man of science, was mocked during the final days of his life. His
colleagues saw him as responsible for the creation of these unprin-
cipled businessmen who preyed on the desperate and elderly; the
editorial writers and cartoonists poked fun at his own elderly condition and its relationship to sexual rejuvenation and masturbation.

In retrospect, Brown Sequard was a pioneering physiologist,
neurologist, and endocrinologist, and much of what he discovered
at the end of the 19th century led to the isolation of this "elixir of
life" almost fifty years later. In 1935 a team of European researchers
isolated the testicular hormone in pure crystalline form; they labelled it testosterone.

While writing this book I wondered whether I should follow in
the footsteps of Brown Sequard to find out what effect taking testosterone might have on me. I spoke with my doctor about the possibility, and he agreed to prescribe testosterone for me on an experimental basis, provided that I sign a waiver absolving him of any
liability. I had imagined taking a few small pills each day, but when I
learned that the only way to take testosterone was to receive a deep
intrasmuscular injection in the buttocks or to wear a scrotal patch,

my enthusiasm waned. And when my wife admitted that she wasn't really keen on risking a return to the tumultuous days of my mid-twenties, the project was shelved. In any event, there is enough evidence to suggest that my physical responses would probably not have been markedly different from those of Dr. Brown Sequard: increased strength, improved recovery after exercise, increased sexual interest—and, of course, a marked lengthening of the arc of my urine. But the more difficult question, especially for my wife, is whether I might have regressed to the emotional state of so many males in their teens and twenties—quick to aggress, domineering, irritable, and horribly competitive.

The History of Testosterone

The history of testosterone begins with Aristotle, who wrote some 2,500 years ago of the effects of castration in his *Historia Animalium*. He realized that the testes were related to the sexual characteristics and the reproductive capacity of the male after watching castrated young male birds that never developed the singing characteristic of adulthood or the desire to attach to a female. In his corresponding observations of the castration of human beings, Aristotle pointed to the high-pitched voice of childhood that persisted into adulthood and the lack of sexual hair.

But it was not until about a hundred years ago that scientists realized testosterone was one of many substances that are secreted internally, in this instance from the testes. In the mid-1850s Claude Bernard demonstrated that the liver secreted glucose directly into the blood, and shortly after the turn of the century D. H. Starling proposed that the word "hormone" be used to identify those internal "chemical messengers" that exerted their effects at some distance from their source. The word *hormone* is derived from the Greek *hormaein,* meaning "to set in motion." A hormone sets in motion or regulates some critical function of the body; there are, among others, sex hormones (for example, androgens and estrogens), thyroid hormones, pituitary hormones, and adrenal hormones.

The question is whether the male hormone testosterone is tied to male aggression. With mice the evidence is very clear. If male mice are castrated within six days of birth, they display very little aggression towards other males, even if they are given doses of testosterone when they become adults. If, however, they are given doses of the male hormone at birth and are later castrated, they still display the aggression typical of adult male mice.

Similarly, if female mice are given the male hormone at birth, they will become more aggressive as adults. This pattern isn't seen consistently with all female animals, however. Female rats exposed at birth to the male hormone do not become aggressive, whereas female cows and goats exposed to the hormone at birth do.

But what happens with human beings? Popular culture tells us that testosterone is strongly implicated in the excesses of male sexuality and, even more critical for public safety, in the genesis of male violence. Critics of male aggression often point to the "testosterone-soaked male psyche"; sociobiologists nod knowingly of the impact that a postpuberty rush of testosterone has on the behaviour of young males.

Log on to an Internet search engine and type in the word *testosterone.* You'll find thousands of potential matches. Within the first ten site descriptions there are several intriguing possibilities. "Pure

Testosterone" promises a "feeling that you get only on those rarest of occasions." Sex or violence or both? The creators of this site are careful to add, "Sorry, ladies, this seems to be designed for hormone pumping teenage boys." The product offered is a computer game called "Warhawk—one smooth flight/war simulator."

Another of the top ten Web sites establishes a putative link between testosterone and the Ladies Professional Golf Association. The point to be made: "half the players on the LPGA tour are leaking testosterone all over each other." These are women who appear to be too manly, at least to the creator of this Web site.

So popular culture tells us that testosterone is related to sex drive and to male aggression. The Internet and its thousands of Web sites are generally in agreement. More testosterone equals more sex, and more testosterone equals more violence.

Testosterone and Sex Drive

The evidence for a link between testosterone and physical strength or testosterone and sexual interest is much stronger than the testosterone-aggression link. If a physician gives a very active middle-aged or elderly man daily or even weekly injections of testosterone, the middle-aged or elderly man will notice some changes—most notably, increased physical strength, increased sexual interest, and more rapid recovery after exercise.

American gerontologist John Morley of Missouri's St. Louis University Medical School has found that active older men who take an oral dose of testosterone improve their strength and their athletic abilities, boost their energy, and improve their moods. Morley suggests that it is important not to give too substantial a dose of testosterone: "Obviously, if you over-treat, you're going to have all these males acting like teenagers again, and we don't need that."

In addition, testosterone replacement therapy can increase sexual interest in hypogonadal men who are impotent. A recent survey of nine studies of the treatment of hypogonadal men with testosterone injections concluded that in every instance libido and sexual interest were increased. There is no suggestion in this research literature, however, that aggression, irritability, or hostility is also to be anticipated from these men.

Testosterone and Aggression

What criminologists call the age-crime curve offers fairly persuasive evidence that testosterone underlies male aggression. In the United States, Canada, and Britain, for example, violent crime by young men increases markedly around age 15, reaches a peak before the age of 20, and then falls precipitously to age 30. Once men reach 40 years of age, violent crime becomes a rarity. The graph looks a lot like a mountain peak, rising sharply to a point at age 20 and then falling off again almost as dramatically.

More important, this pattern of male violence can be found in every nation for which reliable evidence is available. The size of the mountain peak varies considerably, of course, according to the number of violent incidents. The age-crime curve for homicides in the United States, for example, resembles Mount Everest; the age-crime curve for homicide in the United Kingdom is about one-tenth the height of the U.S. curve, but it is identical in shape.

The age-crime curve for violence is not a perfect mirror image of male testosterone levels over time, but it is very similar. Testosterone levels peak shortly after age 20, but the greatest surge in testosterone levels occurs during the teen years, the time at which violent crime is also surging.

Moreover, before puberty girls and boys have approximately equal rates of homicide and suicide. But by age 13 male rates of homicide and suicide are twice as high as female rates; by age 16 male rates are four times as high. Hormonal change seems to be better able to explain this gender gap than does the claim that there is some universal pattern of socialization in every culture past and present that promotes the development of violence in male adolescents.

But the connection between testosterone and male violence is not easy to discern. Researchers have investigated the effects of the hormone when it is administered in different settings. They have given men increased doses of testosterone and monitored the consequences; they have studied the testosterone levels of violent and nonviolent men; and they have looked at changes in behaviour after clinicians have chemically and surgically castrated violent offenders. In all of these circumstances, despite the beliefs within popular culture and the high levels of violence exhibited universally by young men, the research data show something short of a causal connection between testosterone and aggression.

The Effects of Increasing Testosterone

A group of researchers in Scotland gave one sample of fifteen male volunteers testosterone injections weekly for four weeks; another fifteen young men were given injections of a placebo for a similar period of time. The research team asked both groups of men to rate their irritability, readiness to fight, and tendency to become angry. The team found that increases in testosterone did not correspond with any perceived changes in these factors.

But the researchers were studying young men who already possessed relatively high levels of testosterone, not middle-aged or elderly men—and the doses of testosterone that they received were well below the doses typically taken by strength athletes. In a recent study of strength athletes (bodybuilders and weightlifters) a group of British psychologists concluded that self-rated aggression can increase dramatically when men use anabolic steroids. Generally prohibited in athletic competitions, anabolic steroids are modified forms of the hormone testosterone that promote both anabolic (growth-promoting) changes and androgenic (masculinizing) changes.

In this British study researchers contacted a group of steroid users—strength athletes who had been self-administering steroids for between one and five years. They compared three steroid-using strength athletes with three non-steroid-using strength athletes and found that two of the three steroid users reported increased hostility; all three users also reported an increased feeling of power, a gain in strength, and pain in their joints.

This study had two important limitations that are common in studies of the effect of anabolic steroids on aggression. First, there were only six subjects in this study, and they were not, in any sense, a random group drawn from the general population. They represented, rather, that relatively small number of people who engage in a competitive regime of weightlifting. It cannot be assumed that this group of individuals is representative of all individuals who might receive daily injections of testosterone; strength athletes might already be a good deal more aggressive than most of us.

Second, there is the possibility that expectations of effects influenced the outcome of the study. Three bodybuilders who knew that they were taking anabolic steroids were compared with three bodybuilders who knew that they were not. It is well known that a person's expectations can work, at least in the short term, to produce the desired effect. There is, for example, a widespread belief in our culture that testosterone is a precursor of violence and that those who take anabolic steroids are likely to become aggressive or even violent. Thus, the subjects taking steroids might have reported increased hostility because they expected to become more aggressive.

But the bodybuilders were also taking much higher doses of testosterone than subjects in the Scottish study. The British researchers who studied the three steroid users in a London gym concluded that steroid consumption not only improved performance in competitive sport but also changed mood and behaviour.

There are cultural reasons for suggesting that anabolic steroids cause antisocial aggression. Taking steroids is seen as cheating and is subject to penalty in virtually every major sport. Research that suggests or confirms negative consequences for taking steroids will receive cultural support; research that does not sound alarms about taking these hormones is out of step with the public mood.

Researchers who fail to establish a connection between anabolic steroids and aggression or physical harm are usually ignored or marginalized in some other way. If the taking of testosterone to boost competitiveness is to be successfully demonized, the public must believe that consumption is invariably physically and socially harmful—harmful to the individual and to the community.

Vancouver physician and addictions expert Doug Coleman cautions that the research to date on testosterone's ability to produce aggressive behaviour is not conclusive. Researchers have rarely employed double-blind controls and have rarely considered more than a quadrupling of the level of testosterone as an experimental manipulation. Because of the perceived risk of harm to the individual, no ethical approvals would be given for a double-blind study that permitted daily injections of extremely high doses of testosterone. The net result is that even though many strength athletes are taking very high doses of testosterone and reporting increased aggression, researchers cannot be sure that there is a connection between testosterone and aggression.

Men with High Levels of Testosterone

For the past fifty years researchers have also considered the possibility that there are naturally occurring high-testosterone males, who, as a consequence of this hormonal abundance, are more prone to violence than low-testosterone males. One of the more intriguing studies took place among the !Kung, hunter-gatherers of the Kalahari desert—the bushmen of Namibia. From the outset Austrian biologists Kerrin Christiansen and Eike-Meinrad Winkler realized that aggression was an indelible part of social interaction among the !Kung, as suggested by the substantial number of wounds and scars on the heads of their male subjects. The researchers concluded that only a very small percentage of these injuries could have been inflicted by accident (for example, by rolling into the night fire while sleeping).

In the summer of 1987 the research team travelled to Namibia to interview 114 !Kung men, who ranged in age from 18 to 38. The !Kung live with women in small relatively permanent camps, relying on hunting and agriculture for their subsistence. Their contact with Western culture has increased in recent years, and schools and a stable water supply have been developed through government funding. Alcohol has been brought to the !Kung by a range of traders, and it is also brewed indigenously.

The researchers asked the !Kung about what usually caused fights and about how much alcohol they drank. The researchers also took body measurements and blood and saliva samples of testosterone from each of the 114 men. The results showed that men who drank alcohol or who were larger and more robust than the other men were more likely to be involved in violence.

The reasons for the violence usually had to do with women and adultery, though there were also physical disputes over food or money. Once again, sexuality was at the core of male violence. In most circumstances the fights started suddenly, with the throwing of a punch, a stick, or a stone. The fights also ended quickly. The aggressor and victim were usually male, though women were also involved, almost always as victims. About one-third of the !Kung men had fresh wounds or scars as reminders of these encounters.

These 37 were labelled as aggressive, and their levels of testosterone were compared with those of the 77 !Kung who displayed no evidence of such conflict. The results revealed no significant

relationship between either blood or saliva measures of testosterone and evidence of violence. The researchers also referred to
a body of research indicating that high levels of testosterone are
not confined to men who have exhibited violent behaviour. In almost thirty studies researchers have tried to relate blood and saliva
samples of testosterone to various measures of aggression. The
subjects of these studies have been violent offenders, mentally disturbed inmates, and volunteers. The measures of aggression employed by researchers have also varied and have included ratings
of aggression as determined by a psychometric test, peer ratings,
criminal records, self-ratings of aggression, and the presence of
wounds or scars.

Although some of these studies have shown that there is a relationship of statistical significance between testosterone and the
expression of violence, the connection is far from causal. The pre-
diction of which young male might or might not be aggressive, based
on levels of blood or salivary testosterone, would be scientifically
and morally unsound.

The results of research on violent offenders incarcerated in
penitentiaries are also not overwhelming. The most commonly
cited work is that of two American psychologists, L. E. Kreuz and
R. M. Rose, who studied twenty-one male prisoners in the late
1960s, relating blood testosterone levels to individual assaultive-
ness and aggression, as measured by various pencil-and-paper
tests. The researchers found no significant relationship between
testosterone and current levels of aggression. But they did find that
prisoners with a history of violence in adolescence had higher
testosterone levels than those who were not aggressive as adoles-

cents. They interpreted their data to mean that high testosterone levels play a permissive role in the development of aggression during adolescence. But high-testosterone adolescents are no more likely to be aggressive than low-testosterone adolescents— and research since the 1960s has not distinguished between violent offenders and control groups on the basis of testosterone levels.

In the late 1970s British psychologist Rhys Matthews conducted a study of male prisoners based at the notorious Wormwood Scrubs Prison. Matthews selected eleven men with a history of violent crime and matched them with another eleven prisoners for age, height, weight, and amount of time spent in prison. The only clear difference between the two groups of prisoners was that those in one group had multiple previous convictions for crimes of violence. In addition, they had all been cited by police or prison authorities as "being of a violent disposition." In contrast, the eleven nonviolent convicts had no record of violent crime and no police or prison record of aggressive tendencies. The results revealed no relationship between testosterone levels and "being of a violent disposition."

But perhaps researchers have looked at the relationship between testosterone and aggression in too restrictive a framework. Psychologist John Archer and others have suggested that testosterone rises and falls as aggression rises and falls. Early research in this area considered the question of how competitive encounters influence testosterone levels. One study of testosterone levels before and after a tennis match found that testosterone increased with victory and decreased with defeat. Similarly, a study of wrestlers found that the winners of bouts had higher testosterone readings than the losers, but only in the ten minutes after the fight.

A Spanish research team took up this challenge in the mid-1980s with fourteen young male judo competitors. They took blood testosterone levels ten minutes before and after workouts, putting their subjects through two quite different procedures. The first procedure was five minutes of vigorous physical exercise; readings of testosterone were taken before and after this short workout. A few days later the subjects returned and engaged in competitive fighting for five minutes; again, readings of testosterone were taken.

When the results from all subjects were compared, the researchers found that simple exercise increased testosterone levels more than competitive fighting. Winning or losing a specific competitive fight was relatively unimportant. In sum, the relationship between individual testosterone levels and aggression or violence does not seem to be very strong. Researchers who believe in a link between testosterone and aggression have re-interpreted these relatively negative results in a positive light, constructing hopeful hypotheses for future research. Those who do not believe in a link between testosterone and violence view the findings of the research as confirmation of their beliefs.

The Effects of Removing Testosterone from Violent Men

Finally, some studies have looked at what happens when testosterone is removed from violent men. The results suggest that removing testosterone reduces sexual ability and interest, but not aggression or violence.

In the earliest studies in this realm, neurosurgery was performed to remove an area of the brain thought to be responsible for sexual violence. A drill was used to penetrate the skull in order to cauterize the relevant section of the amygdala. (The production of testosterone has been shown to be reduced by amygdalotomy. Removal of the amygdala tends to reduce fear and aggression in all species, including humans.) Unfortunately, an amygdalotomy has no reliable precision, although it has been used in several countries. We have learned from these drilling sessions that there is no part of the brain wholly responsible for aggression or violence that can be neatly excised.

The Edinburgh Amygdalotomy Project was a study of eighteen patients (thirteen males and five females) ranging in age from 8 to 46. In all instances the reason for referral to surgery was "behavior disorder and resulting severe social disruption with varying degrees of aggressiveness." When the amygdala was stimulated with a probe during surgery the patients exhibited a wide range of responses: aggression, threats of violence, anxiety, fatigue, confusion, upper-limb movement, flushing, and disorientation. Bilateral removal of the amygdala was the surgery performed on the eighteen patients. Physician Edward Hitchock set out the less than dramatic benefits that resulted for these eighteen patients.

> In a subgroup of patients who were epileptic, male, with a mental age of more than 6 years, living at home, and with the aggressive behaviour confined to the home situation, the prognosis following amygdalotomy was favourable.

A review of fifty-eight patients undergoing amygdalotomy between 1963 and 1973 revealed that less than 50 per cent reported improvement in control of aggression. Whatever success was achieved with a minority of patients appeared to be attributable to the general "sedative" effect of this kind of neurosurgery. When aggression was diminished, other personality attributes were typically altered, since removal of the amygdala can affect patterns of sleep and feeding and emotional stability.

Castration, whether chemical or surgical, is the more common testosterone-reduction strategy; both types usually diminish or eliminate sexual drive. There is a considerable amount of data from Germany, Switzerland, and Czechoslovakia on the surgical approach; other studies examine what happens when anti-androgens, drugs that lower testosterone, are administered regularly. Anti-androgens have less finality than castration; they also produce unpleasant side effects (breast enlargement, loss of body hair, weight gain, and drowsiness), and they are only effective as long as the subject takes the required drug.

A 13-year-old boy who had committed two serious sexual assaults on little girls had caused severe physical injuries to both of them. The boy was mildly mentally handicapped and came from a very troubled family. The following clinical narrative describes what happened when he was given anti-androgens:

> He was prescribed intermittent bursts of oestrogen derivatives for 20 months as well as oral thioridazine. [This] reduced his sexual drive so very markedly that he had no desire for heterosexual experiences. His assaultive sexuality had been so intense without sex suppressive medication he would have had to be placed in a closed security institution. He matured to some degree and acquired better control of his sexual drives. . . . He now commits thefts instead of sexual offences.

Anti-androgen therapy reduces sexual interest and thereby reduces the risk that an offender will commit future sexual crimes. But it does not reduce antisocial or violent behaviour. Even within prisons, many offenders resist taking these drugs and usually have the civil right to refuse treatment. After release to the community the offender becomes more difficult to monitor and the unpleasant side effects—drowsiness, weight gain, and breast growth—create an incentive for avoiding medication. Compliance is, therefore, a major obstacle both inside and outside prison, especially when male libido will fully return in less than three weeks after use of anti-androgens has been halted.

The most successfully used anti-androgen is MPA—medroxy-progesterone acetate—which can be given in the form of tablets. When given at low doses both testosterone and sex drive diminish, but some amount of sexual activity can be maintained; at high doses the drug is equivalent to a functional but reversible castration.

Reinhard Wille and Klaus Beier of Germany's University of Kiel published a 1989 review article in the *Annals of Sex Research* looking at the accumulated global research to date on the effectiveness of both chemical and surgical castration. The authors dispel a common myth about the consequences of castration. Although spontaneous erection never occurs again after "the operation," erections can occur after intensive stimulation, and even ejaculation is possible in almost one-third of all cases. But all of those castrated have reduced sexual interest and activity, reduced erotic fantasies, and reduced sexual capability.

In the past twenty years castration of sex offenders has been practised only—and rarely—in Switzerland, Germany, and Czechoslovakia. Castrations in Germany have required an application by the patient and an approval by a "castration committee" composed of one lawyer and two physicians. Wille and Beier compared a representative group of 104 castrated German sex offenders (successful applicants) with a comparable group of 53 noncastrated applicants. The researchers were interested in what they called "the crime prevention effectiveness of the surgery," among other things.

The two groups (castrates and noncastrates) were similar in previous criminal record, age, intelligence, social background, and marital status; each group also shared a desire for surgery. The researchers' findings were consistent with previous studies—the incidence of sex crimes was markedly reduced by castration. Wille and Beier's work revealed a recidivism rate, more than ten years after castration, of 3 per cent for castrated applicants and 46 per cent for noncastrated applicants.

This finding, consistent with results from other studies, suggests that castration may have some use as a preventive treatment. After all, if sexually violent men are rarely a threat once they are castrated, shouldn't more of these potential predators be encouraged to apply for "the operation"?

For nonsexual crimes, however, there is no difference in the recidivism rates for castrated and noncastrated applicants. Most important, the nonsexual crimes of the castrati are as socially destructive—as deserving of imprisonment—as the sexual crimes of the noncastrated men.

Similarly, another study of sex offenders given anti-androgen implants found that although recidivism rates for sexual offences were minimal (in contrast to those of control groups), the rate of offending for all other kinds of crime remained unchanged. Researchers have also learned, from studying erectile capability, that although sexual drive is clearly reduced by the anti-androgen MPA, the inappropriate targets of sexual interest do not change (for example, a desire for sex with children).

In sum, research considering the effectiveness of castration and anti-androgens demonstrates quite clearly that sexual ability and interest can be dramatically reduced by castration and similarly reduced, if only temporarily, by anti-androgens. Unfortunately, other antisocial behaviours and the inappropriate desire itself remain intact.

What Is the Link between Testosterone and Aggression?

Canadian psychologist Dave Albert and British psychologist John Archer are probably the world's leading experts on the connection between testosterone and aggression. Albert emphatically rejects the possibility of a link. He argues that there is no clear evidence that increasing testosterone increases aggression, that high-testosterone men are more violent than low-testosterone men, or that aggression or violence increases when testosterone is given to men or women for medical reasons.

John Archer is more cautious in his assessment of this issue—and more hopeful of a link between testosterone and aggression. Archer writes in his review essay "Testosterone and Aggression" that "there is some indirect evidence, but as yet no clear evidence [of effect]." Although he provides data to establish some small correlations between testosterone and aggression, Archer concedes that a cause-and-effect relationship cannot be drawn from available human evidence. He suggests that other measures of aggression may be necessary to tease out the nature of the relationship between the hormone and male behaviour.

There are three arguments that can be levelled against the hypothesis of a testosterone-aggression connection. First, when athletes and others intentionally increase the levels of testosterone in their bodies by a factor of four or more, there are no reliable data to suggest that they become more aggressive. Second, when testosterone levels are increased for medical reasons, for a range of conditions, there are no data to support increased aggression. And third, when violent men and nonviolent men are compared, testosterone does not appear to have any consistent relevance.

But the removal of testosterone by chemical and surgical castration appears to have a significant effect: crimes of sexual violence are markedly reduced. And here is where the connection lies. Testosterone is strongly related to male sex drive; if you take it away, you can expect much less sex, whether of a consenting and loving character or of a kind extracted through violence.

As many feminists have noted, sexual crimes are, most fundamentally, crimes of violence: impositions of power in the highly personal realm of sexuality. The research literature tends to confirm this hypothesis; castration has a marked effect on sexual assault, pedophilia, and transvestitism but appears to have little or no effect on nonsexual crimes, including nonsexual crimes of violence.

Feminists and others have also argued that sex offences are all about power and dominance, not about sex. In this formulation, the incidence of sex crimes shouldn't be affected by castration. But the fact that these crimes are so dramatically affected by castration suggests that sex offences are both about power and dominance and about sex.

If we reflect on testosterone's principal properties—promoting growth and structuring masculinity—it's easy to understand why we might think that this hormone is responsible for sexuality and violence. But testosterone only creates potential; the hormone is like rocket fuel at the point of puberty. It causes erections, nocturnal emissions, and a newfound strength but does not determine how this new potential will be used. If a man takes doses of testosterone and works out regularly, his strength, sexual interest, and mood will improve, as Brown Sequard observed in the late 1880s.

But does testosterone lead to aggression? Two of the world's leading experts, although divided, can find no evidence to support any causal relationship between the two. Testosterone is clearly relevant to understanding male and female sex differences; gonadal secretions of androgens in males are ten times as high as female secretions. At the point of puberty testosterone promotes growth and organizes male sexuality. A template of the male is built, in marked contrast to the template of the female.

Dave Albert is right to insist that widely fluctuating levels of testosterone across various male populations are unrelated to aggression. And he is also correct in claiming that changing normally occurring levels of testosterone will rarely affect aggression. Finally, he is also on solid ground in pointing out that removing testosterone from sexually aggressive men does not change their anti-social conduct.

But the focus of this kind of research diverts us from a clearer understanding of how testosterone and violence are related. We know from the experiences of those who have treated elderly males and hypogonadal men that testosterone can markedly boost sexual interest; this is what Brown Sequard reported, quite correctly, a century ago. But the link between the sexuality that testosterone produces and male violence is more indirect than these research questions suggest.

Why, then, do rates of homicide and suicide double and quadruple, respectively, as testosterone builds in the teenage male? As the teenage male experiences erections and nocturnal ejaculations, he begins to search for an outlet for these new urges. At the same time, he experiences confusion, misunderstanding, and disappointment, in combination with leaving school, leaving home, and trying to support himself—this is what coming of age is so often about.

Testosterone is inextricably tied to male sexuality, and the intensely sexual period of adolescence is when we all begin developing relationships. We are competing with our peers, advertently or inadvertently, for the attraction of potential sexual partners; we learn of betrayal, of unrequited love, and of love lost.

At any age problems with intimate relationships can produce conflict, hostility, and violence. But in adolescence, when testosterone is rushing about the testes and young men are still on a learning curve, the potential for aggression and violence is at its apex. What happens when, in these circumstances, young men experience confusion, misunderstanding, and disappointment? In the absence of corrective influences, it is not surprising that young men express anger, irritability, aggression, and violence.

Testosterone is all about sex. And this is where we find the critical link to male violence. Most male violence is about women. When men kill, they are most likely to kill those they know well, and their single most common victim is a woman with whom they are having an intimate relationship. The perceptions and realities of betrayal, of unrequited love, and of love lost lie behind most homicides.

And so it is when men are at the height of their sexuality, in their teens and twenties, that they are also the most violent. Without testosterone, male violence would be but a sliver of what it is today. It is the testosterone bath in the womb and the testosterone bath at puberty that organize male and female sex differences. And in adolescence, when this hormone is raging through the volatile male psyche, testosterone becomes a potentially lethal factor.

Chapter Six

Environment Matters

My dad molested us three kids, my two older sisters and me.
There was a lot of physical abuse too, but mostly on me.
I had chairs broken over my back, wine bottles whipped at my
head and broken on my back and things like this. I can remember
when I was 11 or 12 thinking, well, it must be great to
grow up and have a couple of kids and you can sleep with them.

DIRK ROCHESTER, CONVICTED MURDERER

W hen I began this project in the early 1990s, I did so because I
wanted to explore biological reasons for the genesis of male
violence. I was not initially convinced, however, that genetics
or the biological differences between men and women could help
to explain a great deal. I would often ask my students to compare
Washington, D.C., and its murder rate of more than 50 killings for
every 100,000 residents, with St. John's, Newfoundland, and its
murder rate of less than 1 killing for every 100,000 residents.

"Is there a higher percentage of males in Washington?" I would ask rhetorically. "I don't think so," I would respond. "If you want to understand the fiftyfold difference between these two cities, biology won't help you. We have to start thinking about cultural differences if we want to comprehend what is going on."

What I said at that time was correct, but, as this book argues, I was only asking one of a number of important questions. If we started with a different inquiry, we would learn that biology is critical to understanding male violence. Why are 9 out of 10 killers in both Washington and St. John's male? And why are some males in both cities more likely to commit violent crime than others?

But the staggering difference between rates of homicide in Washington, D.C., and St. John's, Newfoundland, should not be underestimated. Environment matters a great deal; it is critical to determining how much male violence a given municipality, state, or country will experience. Violence may well always be a male phenomenon, but history tells us that we have the power to diminish—and increase—its incidence.

Rates of Violent Crime

The preceding four chapters have explored biological explanations for the predominance of male violence. This chapter turns to the role of the environment, with specific reference to the past forty years. This span of four decades has been chosen because the data available for this period are more reliable than for any other era. Additionally, analysis of the experiences of the last forty years casts the greatest light on our present circumstances.

Most criminologists consider homicide the best index of violence. Other violent crimes, such as rape, robbery, and assault, are not always reported to the police, and police do not always charge those who commit such criminal offences; discretion in charging is an important and longstanding part of police practice. Moreover, what the police define as an assault, for example, may eventually be characterized by the court as an act of self-defence, or even as an accident—what police initially perceive as a crime may later be defined by a court as innocence or as a failure to establish culpability.

Accordingly, reported crime rates may be inadequate and misleading indicators of the extent of violence in a given society. In some jurisdictions police officers routinely bring all those they believe have committed assaults to the juvenile court for processing. In other jurisdictions police officers act more as keepers of the peace, warning some young men, taking others home to their parents, and ultimately charging some relatively small percentage of the total number of those who commit such acts of violence. For these two types of jurisdictions the real rates of assault may be very similar, but the reported rates will diverge quite markedly. In contrast, almost all killings are discovered by or reported to police and are categorized as such by the investigating police force.

Since the early 1960s there has been a centralized system of data collection in place in the United States, Britain, and Canada. This system shows that since the 1960s, in these three countries, as in all other jurisdictions on earth, past and present, nearly all violence is committed by males. About 90 per cent of murder and robbery suspects and almost 99 per cent of rape suspects are male; these percentages have not changed since the 1960s, and there is no evidence to suggest that any significant change is likely in the future.

A Simple Biological Trigger

The murder rates in the United States, Canada, and Britain were very different from each other in the early 1960s and remain different today—the United States has always had the most lethal violence and Britain the least. In 1962 Britain experienced about 5 homicides for every million members of the population, Canada about 10 homicides, and America about 50. But by 1975, Britain had an annual toll of about 10 homicides for every million Britons, Canada about 25, and America about 100. In the space of a decade, homicide rates had doubled in each of these three countries.

The type of punishment for homicide does not seem to be a factor, since it changed in each country during the 1960s and 1970s, and not all the changes were in the same direction. The U.S. Supreme Court ruled that capital punishment was a cruel and unusual practice in 1967 but reinstated it in 1976, the death penalty remained in place in Canada until 1976, and England abolished capital punishment in the early 1960s.

One explanation for the increase in homicides comes from the realm of biology. Most violence in every society is perpetrated by young males between the ages 15 and 29. If any society experiences an increase in the percentage of its members who are male and between these ages, it can expect a simultaneous increase in violent crime. This is precisely what happened in the United States, Canada, and Britain during the late 1960s and early 1970s. In the decade following World War II all of these countries experienced a baby boom, and the adolescent peak of this boom, with its glut of male teenagers, arrived between 1966 and 1975.

About 70 per cent of homicides are committed by young men under the age of 30. In the mid-1970s the percentage of young men in the populations of the United States, Canada, and Britain increased by about 50 per cent from the levels of the early 1960s. The expected result would be a 35 per cent increase in each country's homicide rate during the late 1960s and early 1970s.

Changes in Women's Roles, Shifting Sexual Mores, and the Pill

But demographic change, rooted in biology, explains less than half of the increase in homicide rates that occurred between 1966 and 1975 in Canada, Britain, and the United States. Another factor was the family disintegration, unparalleled in the preceding two hundred years, that occurred in the late 1960s and early 1970s in the industrialized West.

More than 70 per cent of all killings in the United States, Canada, and Britain take place among people who know each other well. This was true in the early 1960s and remains so today. Such killings, known as primary homicides, are acts of passion committed with the intent to cause serious injury or death. There has been no marked increase in the number of serial killings, mass murders, or even stranger-on-stranger homicides relative to the total number of homicides in any of the countries.

At the turn of the 20th century the relatively novel social arrangement of the industrial nuclear family (a 19th-century creation) was the norm in Britain, the United States, and Canada. The husband and father worked outside the home to bring home a wage (or profit), and the wife and mother worked inside the home, doing domestic chores, bearing and raising children, and providing for the emotional needs of family members. Men secured economic survival for their wives and children; women were committed to hearth, home, and husband.

Although this division of labour and responsibility did not completely unravel until after World War II, social life began to change shortly after World War I, fuelled by the suffragette movement and the war. World War I had required women to contribute in factories and on or near the battlefields, and these contributions gave substantial force to the arguments that advocates of women's rights had been making for more than fifty years. In the decade following World War I, Britain, Canada, and the United States all passed legislation giving women the right to vote. At the turn of the century the participation of women in the labour force had been just under 20 per cent of the working population; after World War I the figure rose to a little more than 20 per cent, and thereafter participation began a slow but steady climb to a little more than 30 per cent in 1961. Almost all of these women were single; even in 1951 only 11 per cent of married women were working outside the family home. But the change was beginning.

In the late 1960s and early 1970s married and single women entered the world of work in unprecedented numbers, doubling their participation in the labour force in a single decade. In the law schools and medical schools of Britain, Canada, and the United States the composition of graduating classes changed. In the decade between the mid-1960s and the mid-1970s, the percentage of women in these professions doubled and in most instances tripled.

At the same time, a postwar ideology was developing in which sex was considered natural and enjoyable for both men and women, and pleasure, more generally, was cast as a worthy pursuit (although there was also a good deal of reaction against this idea). As a result, the age of first sex declined in Britain, Canada, and the United States during the 1950s. Increasing social acceptance of alcohol displaced the Victorian ideology of temperance (soon there would be cannabis and more); the highly sexualized blues of Elvis Presley captivated the young in North America and Britain; the Rolling Stones and many others would later build on these sentiments with albums such as *Sticky Fingers*.

The development of the birth control pill in the early 1960s was a technological breakthrough for women that allowed sexual intercourse without a significant risk of pregnancy and thus ushered in a new era in sexual relations. Within a few years of the introduction of the pill, young men and women in the United States, Canada, and Britain were publicly urging sexual liberation. The popular slogan "Make love, not war" was symbolic of the new possibilities in sexual relationships that the new birth control technology had made possible, changing conceptions of monogamy and commitment in heterosexual relationships.

In the late 1960s and early 1970s, the increased participation of women in the labour force, shifting sexual mores, and the new birth control technology meant that women were no longer sexually or economically dependent on a single male. This new independence produced conflicts in intimate relationships. The divorce rate, an important index of conflict between men and women, quadrupled. Throughout the population in Britain, the United States, and Canada, but especially at its social and economic margins, these cultural changes led directly to an increase in violence. Divorce and estrangement are almost always linked to conflict, misery, and bitterness, but when the participants have few resources and few social skills, the likelihood of an extreme response increases markedly.

Interviews with homicide offenders in prison demonstrate this pattern of behaviour. Kevin Bourne's case is one typical example. He and his wife, Joyce, didn't have many social skills or resources. They were constantly drinking excessively, fighting, splitting up, and then getting back together. Kevin beat a man Joyce was seeing; he also beat Joyce very badly on another occasion, punching her and kicking her, and was charged with assault. In their final effort at reconciliation, Kevin was sitting at home with their two children, waiting for Joyce to arrive. She was late, and as time went by, he became more and more angry, feeling more and more betrayed. He phoned the welfare office and told them to come and take the children, but because it was in the evening few staff members were available and no one came. Kevin Bourne walked to a nearby mall and then returned to their apartment, pacing feverishly. Finally, he decided on his revenge. He placed a pillow over the faces of his sleeping infant daughters, smothering both of them. The notes he left for his wife at the scene of the murder read "I hope you're happy now" and "You don't have to worry about me and the kids."

Ben Costello and his girlfriend, Alice, were living together when Ben was told by a friend that Alice had been "really going at it last night" with another man; the friend didn't know that Ben and Alice were living together. Ben went home, started drinking, and confronted Alice about her behaviour. "Did you have a good lay?" he asked her.

When she started laughing, Ben Costello said that he "just flipped right out." He grabbed a butcher knife from the kitchen and stabbed her. She died the next day in hospital.

And then there was Victor Morrison. His wife told him that she was leaving him for another man, who was younger, more attractive, and more athletic than Victor. Morrison was crushed. "If you love a woman and you've lived with her for twenty years and gone through hard times and gone through good times and raised a fine son and had everything that married people in Canadian society expect you to do, naturally you miss your wife."

After slashing the tires and smashing the windshield of the new boyfriend's car, Morrison finally resolved to give his wife a final separation of his own choosing. He purchased a .357 magnum and went to see his wife at her workplace. "I'll give you a fucking divorce you won't forget," he told his wife and shot her in the chest. She fell face forward to the floor, and he pumped the remaining bullets into her already lifeless body.

Kevin Bourne, Ben Costello, and Victor Morrison were all men with few resources and fewer social skills. When their relationships fell apart they were unable to walk away from the conflict.

Feminism

There is now an abundant literature that blames feminism for the changes of the past generation. Men's rights advocates such as

Robert Bly and Warren Farrell have argued that the new dynamics in male-female relationships have deprived men of their masculinity, increasing male violence. Farrell, for example, argues that murder, rape, and spousal abuse are manifestations of hopelessness—crimes committed by increasingly impotent men. In his words, these offences are "but a minute's worth of superficial power to compensate for years of underlying powerlessness." Bly's and Farrell's arguments are especially interesting given that both men began their careers as male supporters of feminism.

Robert Bly is probably the best known of the men's movement advocates. Bly came of age as a Berkeley peace activist and poet in the 1960s, blasting the Vietnam War in his acceptance speech for the National Book Award. He also conducted "Great Mother" conferences for men and women, where he urged men to embrace their feminine side.

In the 1980s a rather different Robert Bly emerged, complaining about "missing contact with men" and suggesting that for men in American culture "what is missing is the masculine." To make up for these absences, Bly has conducted weekend seminars for men entitled "Love, Sex and Intimate Relationships," urging them to get in touch with the masculine side of their beings.

At the heart of these events is the imagery of the story of Iron John, Bly's best-selling interpretation of a Grimm fairy tale. In this story a boy's mother has imprisoned a hairy wild man in a cage. In metaphorical terms the boy must take back control from his mother by stealing the key from her, opening the cage, and letting the wild man out.

There is a lot of noise and emotion at Bly's events. Writers Steve Chapple and David Talbot describe a "Love, Sex and Intimate Relationships" weekend in California:

> Men young and old are beating drums and wailing about the fathers they never knew. They are laying bare their deepest shame and, more than a little bit, heaping scorn on the dominating women in their lives. Surprisingly, though, sex is not at all a hot topic at these gatherings. The New Man seems infinitely more fascinated with himself than with the ladies.

Like Robert Bly, Warren Farrell was, during the late 1960s and early 1970s, a strong supporter of the women's movement. Farrell wrote a celebrated book, *The Liberated Man,* in support of feminism; he was even described in one publication as "the Gloria Steinem of Men's Liberation." Farrell's view today is that women, notably professional women, are oppressing men. He complains that his ex-wife makes a quarter million dollars a year at IBM—that women can be successful or unsuccessful and still get love. A man, however, must be both good-looking and successful.

Some authors have suggested that men's movement advocates such as Farrell are perpetuating a war against women, using their commentaries to justify the increased violence that women (and men) have been experiencing since the late 1960s and early 1970s. Rather than accept the sexual and economic autonomy of women in the public world of the workplace, these men hold that feminism is to blame for increasing rates of divorce and family violence.

American feminist Susan Faludi's book *Backlash* depicts the icons of the men's movement as the perpetrators of "an undeclared war against American women." Faludi writes of a backlash against the cultural changes of the late 1960s and early 1970s and identifies a backlash "brain trust," a group of nine "neocons" and "neofems" among whom Farrell and Bly figure prominently.

Equality for women in the United States, Canada, and Britain is far from a reality. About 80 per cent of women who work full-time in the labour force are still to be found in traditional "female" jobs with less than average remuneration; they are sales clerks, secretaries, cashiers, and the like. And in the United States, most particularly, the hard-fought victory for reproductive freedoms, exemplified in the Supreme Court's *Roe v. Wade* abortion decision of 1973, has been constantly under attack.

Further, polls and surveys establish that there is little equality in the home in any of these countries. Women typically shoulder about 70 per cent of household duties, regardless of whether they work in the labour force. The one less-than-inspiring difference is, as Faludi notes, that well-educated middle-class men now *think* they do more to help around the house than men did a generation ago.

The increase in the homicide rate since the mid-1960s has coincided with the blossoming of feminism, and this increase can be traced at least partly to the changes inaugurated by feminism. The rate of femicide (the killing of women) is also higher today than it was in the early 1960s, before these structural changes began to take place.

Men killing men is also more common today than during the early 1960s; men have always been more likely than women to be

the victims of homicides. Although the rate of female killings increased between 1966 and 1975 in Britain, Canada, and the United
States, the rate of male killings rose even more sharply. The patterns of male-on-female homicide and male-on-male homicide are
not markedly different, however; in both circumstances the perpe-
trator and the victim know each other well. These are, in both instances, primary homicides: acts of passion typically directed at
long-term friends or acquaintances. The increasing sexual and
economic autonomy of women has created social conflicts, which,
in turn, have increased male violence.

Men appear to have had much more difficulty coping with the
cultural changes of the late 1960s and early 1970s than women
have. The recognition of such change, of a loss of control, of having to adapt, of evolving expectations—these things are all more
threatening to men than to women. (They are, after all, the ones
who are losing some measure of power.)

Most attacks on the women's liberation movement blame feminism, rather than the male response to feminism, for creating
conflict and division between men and women, even though there
is no singular feminism and no singular women's liberation movement. At a basic level, feminism is about moral, economic, political,
and social equality for women. But as it is practised, in the sleepy
groves of academe and in related environments, it is about "radical
feminists," "traditional feminists," and "antimale feminists." The
spokeswomen for the feminist movement during the past generation—Gloria Steinem, Betty Friedan, Camille Paglia, Susan Brownmiller, Germaine Greer, Carol Gilligan, Susan Faludi, and Naomi
Wolf—are not all on the same page. Betty Friedan has been derided

as a "traditional feminist" and has lashed back at the "radical feminists." Camille Paglia has been denounced by Gloria Steinem and others as an "antifeminist." Recent books by Germaine Greer and Susan Brownmiller have been described by Susan Faludi as "increasingly retrograde fare."

It is probably something of a delight for those opposed to women's liberation to see the conflict within the movement. But how to evaluate all of this sniping? Camille Paglia, for example, typically branded as an antifeminist, was having difficulty establishing an academic career until she turned her substantial verbal and oratorical skills into commercially successful attacks on women she describes as "whining feminists." Paglia has even suggested that if civilization had been left in the hands of women, we'd still all be living in grass huts. But Paglia is a master of tongue-in-cheek overstatement—and an advocate for the tolerance and support of sexual diversity and unfettered choice in the matter of abortion.

A clear understanding of how and why men have become more violent and who is to blame is not likely to be found in the often contradictory voices of the women's movement. These women have made more and sometimes less useful contributions to the interests of equality and the pursuit of social justice for women, but an examination of the strengths and weaknesses of their arguments is not likely to help us here. The more important point to be made, in relation to male violence, is that the increasing sexual and economic autonomy of women has created social conflicts, which, in turn, have increased male violence.

Pornography

Many academics, policymakers, and politicians have pointed to the growth in the pornography industry over the last forty years as a source of increased male violence. Convicted serial rapist and murderer Ted Bundy told reporters before his execution that he could trace his murderous sprees directly to his consumption of explicit sexual materials.

As the sun set on the 1960s, Hugh Hefner was becoming the ever more popular purveyor of *Playboy,* a "men's magazine." Now known as pornography, *Playboy* and its print and video offspring were more than occasionally described fawningly in the mainstream press as "erotica."

In the early 1960s *Playboy* and other magazines had been challenged by prosecutors and politicians for their photographs of topless women. In 1962 criminal charges of obscenity were levelled against D. H. Lawrence's *Lady Chatterley's Lover* for its frank description of sexual intercourse. But public opinion was shifting; there was a male market for photos of nude women, especially in a magazine that espoused an ideology of liberal tolerance. And both men and women, with reliable birth control in place, endorsed a freer sexuality.

In the 1970s and the 1980s the nature of mainstream pornography changed. The topless women yielded to more explicit photographs that showed pubic hair, genitalia, and occasional intimations of violence. Film and video productions documented sexual intercourse from foreplay to ejaculation and orgasm. At the millennium, hundreds of explicit videotapes and photographs are commercially available for adults in virtually every town in the United States, Britain, and Canada. The Internet offers more of the same: photos of naked women, oral sex, group sex, lesbian sex, gay sex, and anal sex.

The audience for the explicit sexual images of print and film is almost exclusively male, and it always has been. Pornography also reflects, certainly at its margins and sometimes at its core, hostility or indifference to the interests of women; it is mostly about male satisfaction and about men viewing women as their sexual chattels. The Internet has, for example, along with the anticipated photo groupings of "hot chicks" and "hot sex," the more disturbing categories of "sluts and bitches."

But pornography is not a major part of the lives of most men in Canada, the United States, or Britain; surveys indicate that less than 10 per cent consume such material in any given year. And although the images have become more explicit over time, there is no compelling evidence that this greater explicitness has actually caused more male violence. Most videotapes in the current market simply display men and women engaging in a variety of sex acts, typically with no meaningful story line. In response to these images (and that breathless salute "You're so big"), the male viewer may become aroused and masturbate, he may be vaguely interested, or he may even be bored. At its best, pornography is a distorted form of sex education; at its worst, it is an appalling waste of time.

With more coercive images, however, pornography is a less benign influence, especially for men at the margins. The statements of Ted Bundy and others suggest that such images may have the capacity to produce a violent reaction in the male viewer. Domestic violence is, after all, relatively common—and images that say that violence against women is acceptable lend support to the predilections and beliefs of angry, misogynist men. Even within this realm, however, it is difficult to separate the inclinations of the viewer from the effects of the images. In any event, prohibition of images that link explicit sex to coercive violence—and do so approvingly—is an appropriate use of the power of criminal law. But mainstream pornography, with its emphasis on genitalia in motion, is not a critical link to understanding increasing violence against women in the postwar era.

Alcohol and Other Drugs

As the rules of social life were changing during the 1960s, the principles of monogamy and self-restraint were losing ground to a young generation that wanted, along with more liberal sexual relationships, more alcohol, additional ceremonial drugs, and very different music. Some of these changes remain with us today; they are a part of our culture. Rock and roll and marijuana have become billion-dollar businesses, and alcohol has comfortably maintained its market share.

From the mid-1960s to the mid-1970s, alcohol consumption increased by 50 per cent per capita in Canada, Britain, and the United States; this increase significantly affected violent crime. Virtually every analysis of domestic assault and homicide points to alcohol abuse as a factor in more than half of all incidents. One study of homicides in Vancouver found that more than half of all perpetrators and all victims had blood alcohol levels of more than .16—twice the legal level of impairment—at the time of the crime.

Similarly, a study of homicide in Copenhagen, Denmark, looked at 251 cases of homicide between 1959 and 1983. The authors noted that the homicide rate had increased approximately 100 per cent during those years, as had the rate of alcohol consumption. Alcohol abuse and intoxication were present in more than half of all these cases. A study of 248 homicides in Cape Town, South Africa, in 1990 and 1991 found that more than 50 per cent of victims and perpetrators had blood alcohol levels greater than .10 per 100 millilitres of blood; in other words, more than half of the offenders and victims were intoxicated at the time of the offence. Another study, of homicide offenders in Sweden between 1970 and 1981, found that both offenders and victims were intoxicated in 44 per cent of cases.

This pattern has been prevalent for more than fifty years—for as long as researchers have been gathering data about the relationship between alcohol and violence. It has been seen in South Africa, Sweden, Canada, the United States, France, and Britain—in every Western industrial society in which alcohol has been used. As early as 1945 American criminologist Marvin Wolfgang observed this consistent portrait of victim-offender intoxication at the time of homicide.

Clearly there is a correlation between alcohol intoxication and homicide, but does that mean that there is a cause-and-effect relationship? After all, there are millions upon millions of instances of drunkenness in which no violence takes place. Further, global rates of alcohol consumption do not correlate with global rates of homicide. The French and the Italians consume more alcohol per capita than other nationalities, and yet they are far from having the world's highest homicide rates. That dubious distinction belongs to the United States and South Africa, which finish well down the list in per capita consumption of alcohol.

Much depends on the social circumstances in which intoxication occurs. Professor Roland Gustafson of Sweden's University of Orebro has been studying the link between alcohol and aggression in laboratory experiments for almost twenty years. To date there are three major theories cited in the literature: the disinhibition hypothesis, the arousal hypothesis, and the attentional hypothesis.

The disinhibition hypothesis posits that alcohol weakens or eliminates inhibitions against aggression. According to this line of argument, as alcohol intoxication increases so too should the likelihood of aggression. This reasoning is based on the assumption that intoxication produces aggression, while sobriety acts as a check on aggression. But as Gustafon's research demonstrates, unprovoked intoxicated subjects rarely become angry as a result of drinking alcohol. Other researchers have also shown that intoxicated behaviour is strongly influenced by the social and cultural norms and pressures of the given community. In short, the social circumstances of intoxication are critical to the development of aggression; there is no simple disinhibition effect.

The second hypothesis linking alcohol to aggression suggests that alcohol creates a high level of arousal, which in turn can be interpreted—or misinterpreted—by the intoxicated person as anger or as a state of threat. Again, there is little evidence to support this idea. As with the disinhibition hypothesis, it is clear that alcohol intoxication in itself does not inevitably produce aggression. Additionally, there are other drugs that increase arousal—cannabis, caffeine, and nicotine—but are not linked to increased aggression.

The attentional hypothesis offers the most promising link between alcohol and aggression. An intoxicated person's "attentional capacity," or ability to focus on what is important, is reduced by alcohol consumption, and in circumstances where there is provocation and a restricted range of responses available, an intoxicated person is likely to become aggressive. In virtually every laboratory study where human beings are both provoked and frustrated, alcohol consumption leads to more aggressive responses, provided that an option to aggress is available.

In one experiment, for example, the research subject tries to win a fairly large sum of money; his partner, a confederate (a member of the research team, unknown to the subject), frustrates this objective by performing poorly. The subject can either administer shocks of increasing frequency in an effort to compel better performance from his partner or simply flick a switch to light a lamp that gives feedback. If the subject is given alcohol, along with the frustration of his confederate's poor performance, the number and intensity of shocks inevitably increases. When cannabis is substituted for alcohol, there is no increase in the number or intensity of shocks given to the confederate; high doses of THC, the active ingredient in marijuana, tend to decrease aggression towards a confederate.

In other words, alcohol, our culture's legal drug of choice, can facilitate aggression and violence in social circumstances where there is provocation and frustration and where an aggressive response is presented as an option or is understood to be appropriate. When human beings live in social situations where provocation and frustration are the routines of daily life—and where aggression is seen as an appropriate response—alcohol is like gasoline to a fire.

In the ghettos of Chicago, Detroit, and countless other American cities, where provocation, frustration, and alcohol abuse are commonplace, homicide rates are five to twenty times as high as the national rate. The same is true in London's Brixton, certain suburbs of Paris, and Vancouver's downtown east side. In similar places throughout the world, hundreds of thousands of men live with frustration and see aggression as a reasonable response to the various provocations of social interaction. These are our repositories of male violence, and the most important chemical trigger in these circumstances is not testosterone but alcohol, the world's most popular psychoactive drug.

One example is provided by Scott Millar, a disadvantaged man with a history of involvement in crime. He is now serving time for a crime triggered by alcohol. Interviewed after his conviction, he explained that the violence began while he was drinking heavily with another young man who had served time with him during a previous prison stint. The young man, who was very drunk, said to Millar, "I'm going to tell your old lady you fucked me in the ass when you were in prison." Millar threatened to "punch his head in" if he didn't shut up.

The young man was staggering and laughing when he picked up Millar's loaded gun. He started dialing the phone, saying that he was going to call Millar's parents and tell them about the sex in prison. Millar was furious and lunged at him. The two men fought over the gun and it went off; the bullet travelled through the young man's nostril, killing him instantly. This is a very common type of homicide: two men, intoxicated by alcohol, settling a dispute.

Violence by women is also strongly influenced by alcohol abuse. Criminologist Barry Spunt and his colleagues interviewed 215 female homicide offenders in the 1980s, asking them about the circumstances of their crimes, their motivations for killing, and the role of legal and illegal drugs in their lifestyles. Spunt and his colleagues found that more than half of the women's homicides could be classified as driven by alcohol. The women told those who interviewed them that they were much more likely to kill because they were out of control with alcohol than for any other reason.

Illegal Drugs, Guns, and a Criminal Lifestyle

Since the late 1960s the industries of illegal-drug distribution (principally marijuana, but also cocaine and other stimulants and the opiates) have expanded exponentially; we have returned, in form and substance, to the time of American Prohibition, that period between 1920 and 1933 when alcohol was criminally prohibited.

The homicide rate in the ten-year period before Prohibition averaged 6.1 per 100,000 Americans; during the thirteen years of Prohibition the death toll jumped to an average of 8.3 per 100,000, only to fall to 6.5 in the ten years following Prohibition. To put this in more concrete terms, in the ten years before Prohibition there were about 7,000 killings annually in the United States, during Prohibition about 10,000 each year, and in the ten years following about 7,000 each year.

For the past thirty years, large illegal-drug industries have been operating in much the same manner as the bootleggers of Prohibition, without any form of regulation. The illegal-drug dealer cannot use administrative or constitutional law to compel ethical conduct from his associates. And in a relatively small number of buy-sell transactions, violence is the consequence of society's failure to provide a legitimate mechanism of regulation.

Ian Blenheim and Danny Harrigan are good examples of this kind of violence. The two men were involved in an outlaw motorcycle club, and there was a dispute within the biker community over the conduct of a man involved in the illegal distribution of amphetamines. Blenheim and Harrigan went over to the man's house with a friend, hoping to work things out. But the speed dealer pulled out a gun the moment they walked in and began firing. Ian Blenheim also had a gun, however, and his shot connected first. The dealer was hit in the head, and a second man in the room went running for a shotgun. But Blenheim shot him before he could reach it. Harrigan stabbed a third person, a female witness. Within minutes, three people were dead and Harrigan and Blenheim fled the scene. Violence had become their mechanism for resolving disputes.

The link between prohibition of drugs and increased violence is another part of the puzzle of increasing male violence over the last thirty or forty years. Illegal-drug industries expanded in Canada, the United States, and Britain at the same time that homicides began to increase, and in certain sections of many cities in the United States, killings related to the drug trade now constitute a majority of all homicides, although they typically amount to less than a third of the national total.

But one-third of all killings is a statistic of consequence. Some of the more specific examples are alarming. In 1953 there were 321 homicides in New York City. In 1993, although the population of the city had declined, there were 1,665. In 1953 there were 82 homicides in Los Angeles County; in 1992, with a doubling of the population, there were more than 2,500. In many other American cities the portrait of male violence is similar; there has been more than a 500 per cent increase in the rate of killing over the past forty years. It seems clear that although homicide rates have doubled across America during this time, the increases in the urban United States have been even more substantial. In fact, even in Britain and Canada, it appears that the highest homicide rates are to be found in large urban settings.

In the United States, in cities such as New York, Los Angeles, and Detroit, members of a historically oppressed underclass have become involved in illegal-drug dealing, often backed by guns. As a result, some urban homicide rates are more than double the national average. And the growth of suburbia—as the American middle class flees the city for the safety of bedroom communities—has fuelled the increase in urban violence. The inner cities have, until relatively recently, simply been left to disintegrate.

The annual reports of homicide for 1998 point, in absolute terms, to more than 20,000 killings in the United States in 1998, about 650 in Canada, and about 650 in Britain. In the United States, the growth of a culture of handgun violence in the inner cities and the presence of a substantial historically oppressed minority (20 per cent of the population) have contributed to male violence.

In 1998 more than ten thousand Americans were killed with handguns, about 50 per cent of all American homicides. In Canada, handguns are used in less than 20 per cent of all homicides and in Britain in less than 10 per cent. It is probably not accidental that the

country with the lowest ratio of handgun homicide to total homicide also has the lowest rate of homicide. Although these weapons
can be associated with relatively peaceful activities such as target
ranges, guns remain symbols of lethal violence, used in film, television, and print to dispense with a villain. And that may be part of
the problem. American iconography promotes the use of these
weapons as a principled solution to the conflicts of social life.

Although not all gun owners represent a risk of violence (less
than 1 per cent of those who own handguns or rifles will ever fire
these weapons at another human being), research shows that gun
ownership is a risk factor. A gun owner's education, resources,
training, and sobriety may make the risk of violent death virtually
nonexistent, but for men at the social margins the risk is not negli-
gible. A study published during the 1990s in the *New England Journal of Medicine* revealed that in the United States homes with guns
were three times as likely to experience a homicide as homes without guns and four times as likely to experience a suicide.

There is also the variable of historically oppressed populations,
especially in Canada and the United States. In Canada about 2 per
cent of all Canadians are indigenous aboriginals, but more than 20
per cent of homicide suspects—and homicide victims—are from
this population. In the United States, although 20 per cent of the
population is black, almost 70 per cent of homicide suspects are
black. In both countries the homicide rate of the formerly colo-
nized population is almost identical; it is only the greater size of the
black population in the United States (20 per cent of the U.S. population, in contrast to 2 per cent of the Canadian population) that
makes race appear to be a more important variable in that country.

It is not race itself, however, that is an important factor. It is the extent to which a person is connected to a social and economic underclass. When these notions are factored into data about homicide, whether a person is black, aboriginal, or white becomes insignificant. The United States has a relatively recent history of enslaving blacks, and Canada has a relatively recent history of oppressing the aboriginal peoples, forcing them into residential schools and outlawing their traditional customs. These conditions of enslavement and oppression have created a social underclass in these two countries. Oppression of the kind experienced by blacks in the United States and aboriginals in Canada spawns resistance, typically self-destructive, in the form of increased rates of homicide, suicide, and family disintegration; male violence increases. In contrast, Britain has no significant underclass that has been systematically oppressed; centuries have passed since feudalism yielded to industrial capitalism and parliamentary democracy. In such circumstances, a less contentious and more civil society has emerged. Homicide rates in Britain remain markedly lower than homicide rates in Canada and the United States.

In the United States today there are neighbourhoods where the use of a gun is associated with the daily business of illegal-drug distribution. These are neighbourhoods with little opportunity, where young men are prepared to use lethal force to attain the products that are symbols of success in American culture. And these symbols take on huge meaning in a culture that worships individual celebrity and individual wealth; the values of community and collective well-being have much less appeal.

Abuse, Neglect, and the Glorification of Male Violence

The men who populate our prisons, reformatories, and penitentiaries are drawn almost exclusively from a class of abused and neglected children. The most critical factor is not that they came
from backgrounds of poverty or unemployment. Newfoundland,
for example, has one of the highest rates of unemployment in the
Western world, but the province also has a lower rate of homicide
than any industrialized democracy in the world.

It is the treatment of children that matters. The files of men
imprisoned in penitentiaries for violent crime are replete with references to backgrounds of physical abuse and emotional neglect.
Tom Pickard, for example, was a heroin user who shot and killed
another user who was trying to take away his drugs. Pickard was
raised by his aunt; there was a lot of drinking in the home and a lot
of violence. "Well, there was physical abuse, there was mental
abuse, and there was sexual abuse when I was younger," he told an
interviewer a number of years ago. "I just never really felt like I ever
belonged anywhere. I guess that's basically something I've come to
realize now. I just never belong."

Louis Fisher had a similar background. His parents separated
when he was four years old, and he never saw much of his father
after that. His mother was described by a neighbour as "an alcoholic of the worst type. She had no control of herself at any time.
The place was nothing but a sex house." In 1960, when he was 24
years old, Louis Fisher stabbed a woman to death; her half-nude
body was found in a parking lot. Similarly, Leonard Peete, a young
man who raped and killed a 70-year-old woman during the late

1970s, described his upbringing as "very unhappy." His mother was a Métis who became an alcoholic when he was very young; his father was a white Catholic and a strict disciplinarian who was consistently physically violent towards his children.

Not all men who are abused will go on to commit violent crime, however, and not all men who commit violent crime will necessarily have a background of abuse or neglect. Kip Kinkel, for example, was the product of an upper-middle-class home in which he suffered neither abuse nor neglect. And there are countless examples of men who have suffered abuse as children and do not repeat this behaviour as adults. But abuse and neglect are significant risk factors; the child who is abused and neglected is more likely to be involved in violent crime than the child who is raised in a more nurturing environment.

Much in our culture also encourages and even glorifies male violence. Every winter morning in Canada and the United States television stations run highlights of the previous evening's hockey games, and among these highlights are a few fights: players punching each other in the head, blood streaming down their faces. Twenty years ago fights were seen as an embarrassment to the game and were rarely featured on the following morning's televised highlights. Now television commentators celebrate the violence: "an excellent tiff," "the highlight of the third period."

So too on the football field—fighting does not mean ejection from the game in either of these sports. Rather, it is celebrated as an expression of machismo. In Britain, with its tradition of soccer hooliganism, the situation is the same. Young men travel to soccer games not to support their team but in the hopes of a showdown with similarly demented fans from the opposing side. Hollywood makes movie after movie and software companies make video game after video game where gunplay or some other kind of male violence is the solution to a given problem. We have made heroes out of Sylvester Stallone, Arnold Schwarzenegger, and many others who are celebrated for their ability to dominate through physical strength and sophisticated weaponry.

It is small wonder that male violence remains a major social problem when millions of dollars are spent annually implicitly endorsing violent behaviour. It is bad enough that sex differences, testosterone, size, speed, and strength, our genes, and our evolutionary history have already combined to make men more likely to inflict pain on other human beings. Now this violence is endorsed on our playing fields, in our stadiums, and on television and movie screens every day of the week.

There have been many environmental triggers for the increase in male violence over the last forty years: men's reactions to feminism and the emerging equality of women; the increased consumption of alcohol; the prohibition of illegal drugs, especially when firearms are a part of doing business; physical abuse and emotional neglect in childhood; and the cultural glorification of male violence, whether in competitive sport or by the male role models of television and film. The next chapter merges biology and environment and considers solutions.

Chapter Seven

Calming the Beast

Rebellious subjects, enemies to peace,
Profaners of this neighbour-stained steel—
Will they not hear? What ho! you men, you beasts,
That quench the fire of your pernicious rage
With purple fountains issuing from your veins,
On pain of torture, from those bloody hands
Throw your mis-temper'd weapons to the ground,
And hear the sentence of your moved prince.

SHAKESPEARE, ROMEO AND JULIET

The day that we brought Emily home began well enough. Rupert, our 4-year-old chocolate Labrador retriever, was curious about, even friendly with, this 6-week-old puppy, nuzzling her and happily chasing her around the lawn. It was only when she began to play with his tennis ball—*his* tennis ball—that he intervened, biting into her muzzle so deeply that blood began to flow.

I scooped up Emily and banished Rupert to the outer garden. Her face was covered in blood and becoming very swollen; she was squeaking with pain. Our trip to the veterinarian was a little tense. Had Rupert fractured her skull? Might she lose an eye? Would she die in my arms before we arrived at the clinic?

The veterinarian immediately took Emily into his examining room and began to dab at the blood as she squeaked and wriggled. He told us that she would probably survive, but he wanted to take some X-rays. Could we get a bite to eat and come back in about an hour?

I looked like a cast member from the set of a slasher film, standing at the door of the restaurant with blood on my shirt and blood on my jeans, but the waitress, displaying a remarkable sangfroid, actually seated us. The rest of the day was much less eventful. Emily survived and has prospered over time, though she is still a little wary of Rupert and his apparently male tendencies. The boy still pads about the house, imagining himself Lord of the Manor, with two and, very occasionally, three tennis balls crammed into his mouth.

It is the old game of dominance and conquest. No metaphorical notches on the bedpost, hot sports cars, or elegant suits for Rupert. Possession of all available tennis balls is the symbol of success in his mind.

But it is possible to calm the beast in Rupert, just as it is possible to calm the beast in males of the human species. There is a lot of work involved with human beings—a lot less with dogs. Rupert, for example, has had his testicles removed, and this has markedly reduced his appetite for senseless violence. This strategy is, however, not usually considered an ethically appropriate response to the senseless violence of teenage boys. Additionally, Rupert views my wife and me as leaders of the pack and therefore as deserving of great devotion. As a dog, he is more than happy to be dependent upon us for his food, entertainment, and recreation. We have taught him to sit, to shake a paw, and not to bite Emily. All of these environmental factors have had a civilizing influence on Rupert.

Environmental factors also present the best hope for calming the beast in human males, but as with dogs, any thoughtful and productive strategy will require excursions into the domain of biology. I have learned that the best explanation for the universal ten-fold difference between men and women in committing violent crime lies in the y chromosome, and further, that the reason some men are violent and others are not also has a good deal to do with their genes. But there remains an unwillingness to accept that male violence flows from an amalgam of genes and environment. Biologists understand male violence through the lens of natural selection, often ignoring environmental explanations as sloppy science, but social scientists are worse. They are the proverbial ostriches, heads well buried in the sand, ignoring the overwhelming weight of scientific data. Despite mountains of evidence, sociologists, social workers, and most psychologists consistently analyze the social world on the assumption that environmental factors are the basis for human behaviour.

This interpretation is a misreading and a misdiagnosis of a very serious social problem. Richard Rhodes's recently published book *Why They Kill: The Discoveries of a Maverick Criminologist* is a good example of this continuing misdiagnosis. Rhodes points to the research of criminologist Lonnie Athens, who argues that brutalization at the hands of parents, husbands, or gang leaders is wholly responsible for male violence. Once again, it is the environment that is to blame. The conservative criminologist James Q. Wilson, critiquing Rhodes's book in the *Manchester Guardian,* provided a much needed balance:

> One reason children differ is that their personalities are different, and many—but not all—of these differences have a genetic basis. Men are vastly more aggressive and violently criminal than are women. Part of this difference may be that boys are more likely to be abused than girls, but it is not likely that this difference can explain why men are at least 10 times as likely as women to be arrested for a violent crime. There is no evidence that they are 10 times as likely to be brutalized.

In criticizing Rhodes's book and in saying that both genes and environment matter, Wilson is the real maverick.

Most attempts to understand violence pay only lip service to the contributions of biology. Clinical psychologists typically look to their theoretical paradigms to understand the origins of such behaviour: Freudians suggest that the id is out of balance, Jungians resort to the collective unconscious, and behaviourists emphasize patterns of negative and positive reinforcement. Courtroom experts point to the life history of the convicted man to help judges and juries understand his violence: his background of abuse and neglect, his failure to complete primary education, his involvement with a subculture of criminal activity, and his failure to hold down a job. Criminal courts virtually never hear of the risks of the Y chromosome and of the genetic risks inherent in the individual before the court. Researchers and policymakers acknowledge that biology has something to do with male violence, but this avenue is never explored, leaving a confused and misled public with the impression that such crime is almost wholly a function of environmental influence—that people are bad because bad things have been done to them.

Solutions for the problem of male violence will, for the most part, be found in the environment and in our culture, but diagnosis of this behaviour must begin to reflect its biological origins—that being male is the most important risk factor for violence and that some men are at much greater risk of violence than others precisely because of their biological limitations. The rest of this chapter looks at specific ways to ameliorate the problem of male violence.

Recognize the Biological Basis of Male Violence

Male human beings are more like male apes than is commonly recognized. Our patterns of violence have always been remarkably similar. Even in the contemporary global context, both male apes and human beings continue to engage in intergroup raiding. The genocides of Rwanda, Kampuchea, and Indonesia and the group murders of blacks, homosexuals, and others in the United States find their equivalent in the behaviours observed among bands of male chimpanzees in the heart of Africa during the past three decades.

Human beings do not come into the world as blank slates. We are male or female, and shades in between, and the limits to our abilities and personalities already reside in our genes. Boys are more physical, more oriented to the spatial, more likely to manipulate their environments, and more likely to hit than girls. Girls are less physical, more verbally oriented, and more inclusive and communal in their styles of play than boys.

The continuing denial of the existence of these sex differences skews our understanding of why men are violent. On Israeli kibbutzim, despite the freedom of access to any occupation, men outnumber women in trades and technical occupations (carpentry, plumbing, and electrical work) by a factor of more than 10 to 1; women outnumber men by a similar margin in elementary school teaching and child care. These roles have not been forced on either gender but have been willingly assumed, in large measure because such inclinations and aptitudes are biologically mediated. The lesson here is simple: let's not try to put a round peg into a square hole or vice versa. And most important, in the context of violence, we should not assume that men and women have similar inclinations, their tendencies mediated only by cultural experiences.

Because of testosterone and biological differences in speed, size, strength, sexuality, spatial skills, verbal skills, and empathy, men are at greater risk than women for becoming violent. As a result, men need to work at something that they are not biologically inclined to do: improving their ability to communicate, to demonstrate empathy for others, and to understand their sexuality and its effect on others. Science writer Robert Pool provides an example of his own recognition that he should change his behaviour:

> The women were all leaning into the table with their eyes on whoever was speaking, while we four males were leaned back in our chairs, looking in various directions—at the wall, at the table, at a spot a few inches over someone's head. We males all

laughed, but I think it made us a little uncomfortable. We didn't want to go back to staring past each other, and we sure didn't want to start looking into each other's eyes, so we made a big joke out of it. One boy turned completely around to face the opposite wall as he talked, the other covered his eyes with his hand, and I stuck my head under the table. It was easier than eye contact.

The social organization of the bonobos points to possible solutions to the problem of male violence. In these apparently non-violent communities of apes, females have more social and political power than in other communities of primates. The males of the band are more responsive to the females of the band than to other males, looking to them for advice and leadership when conflicts arise. It is tempting to suggest, on the basis of this evidence, that men need to be more like women in order to improve their abilities to communicate and diminish their natural tendencies to aggress. We must support the equality of men and women while recognizing the social costs of the biological predispositions of the male. In the realm of violence, male biology confers a handicap. Once we recognize this, we can take a first step towards reducing the conflicts that our genes have created for us.

Understand That There Is an Important Relationship between Sex and Violence

Research reveals that the majority of incidents of male violence, whether directed towards women or other men, are related to sexuality. Most homicides take place among intimates, and sexual jeal-

ousy or infidelity is often at the heart of the anger that motivates
the crime. The age-crime curve is very closely related to the testosterone curve. As testosterone surges through young men's bodies at
puberty, their rates of violent crime increase dramatically. In every
community past and present, young men, in the first few years after puberty, are the most likely of all human beings to be violent.

The connection between testosterone and aggression is not especially strong or direct, but the connection between testosterone
and sexuality is overwhelming. And this is the key to understanding
the connection between testosterone and violence. The increase in
violent crime experienced by most Western cultures in the late
1960s and early 1970s can be linked to sexuality, specifically to the
changing conceptions of monogamy and commitment that produced unprecedented conflict in male-female relationships. After
a generation of stability, rates of divorce increased by about 400 per
cent in the span of a decade.

And when sexual relationships are disrupted, challenged, or
changed, even if for very good reasons, men, especially young men,
do not take this collapse very well. We already know that young
men are at greatest risk of violence when the realities of immature
sexual relationships—confusion, misunderstanding, and disappointment—are in evidence. The increase in domestic homicides
during the late 1960s and early 1970s can be tied to the restructur-
ing of male-female relationships that occurred during that time.
As many evolutionary psychologists and biologists have observed,
societies that place less value on the stability of monogamous
relationships—societies in which there are greater numbers of sin-

gle, separated, and divorced males in circulation—are more dangerous societies. This is clearly the lesson that we can draw from the turmoil of the late '60s and early '70s, a situation that remains with us today.

Our culture expresses much more concern and upset about sex than it does about violence. We are horrified at the prospect that teenagers might watch films featuring explicit sex, but we think little of sending them off to theatres to watch horrific violence. Our public and private schools devote endless amounts of time to discussing the history of warfare, identifying heroes, and celebrating the legitimacy of violence. In contrast, even the suggestion that sexuality could be discussed in an educational setting often spurs righteous indignation.

We need to relax about sexuality and to become a lot more uptight about violence. Until recently only heterosexuality was seen as a legitimate form of sexual expression. Gay men and women were, and in some places still are, targets for ridicule and violence. The brutal murder of Mathew Shepard in Wyoming and the constant harassment and beating of male homosexuals is evidence of fear, transformed into hostility. We need more openness about variations in sexuality and the pleasures that sexuality can bring.

Perhaps once again we should follow the example of the bonobos, the pygmy chimpanzees that live in Africa, south of the Zaire River, which have taken quite a different route from human beings and other primates in relation to violence. There does not appear to be a significant level of violence in their communities, but there is a good deal of sexual behaviour—masturbation, same-sex stimulation, opposite-sex stimulation. The structure of bonobo society is also largely matriarchal. In an atmosphere of less male dominance and a greater relaxation about sexuality, the corollary appears to be less violence.

No one argues that violence is a wonderful activity that brings pleasure to all who participate in it, but we barely give lip service to the idea that sexuality is all about pleasure, and we're not very comfortable with this pleasure—in extolling its virtues, or just talking about it. We even go so far as to criminalize those who wish to sell sexuality. We—well, men especially—would much rather talk about who won the hockey fight in the morning's television highlights than we would talk about sex.

The sexual liberation movement of the late 1960s produced costs and benefits. The costs can be seen in increased rates of divorce and more male violence within intimate relationships. The benefits can be seen in the beginnings of a greater openness about sexuality and in the increasing social and political equality of men and women. If men can cede a greater measure of political, economic, and social control to women, especially in relation to sexuality, male violence will diminish.

Rethink Our Approach to Alcohol and Other Drugs

Intoxication by alcohol is closely related to the problem of male violence. In the past forty years the per capita consumption of alcohol has risen steadily in North America and much of Western Europe, increasing most dramatically at the same time that homicide rates increased most dramatically. In about half of all homicides in Western cultures both victim and offender are legally impaired. Police also implicate alcohol as a critical factor in anywhere from one-half to two-thirds of violent incidents. And when push comes to shove, a faster, stronger, and larger man is more likely to injure; a woman is more likely to be injured.

In circumstances where individuals are provoked, and where an aggressive response is seen as appropriate, alcohol can act as gasoline does to a fire. In social settings where frustration and provocation are routine—in urban ghettos and in families where abuse and neglect are common—alcohol is a very dangerous drug, amplifying the potential for violence. Yet our culture retains an amused tolerance for the ritual of alcoholic excess, evident in literature, television, and film. In addition, advertisements on television and in magazines falsely link consumption of alcohol with access to attractive partners, luxury goods, and pristine wilderness settings.

Cannabis does not appear to be nearly as dangerous as alcohol, either for an individual or for a society. Alcohol can kill a user at a single sitting; cannabis cannot. The ingestion of alcohol is related to violence; the ingestion of cannabis is not. More remarkably, even though cannabis is illegal in most jurisdictions, the price of a cannabis high is typically less than the price of an alcohol high. Cannabis is not a drug that users can only afford if they turn to crime.

Other illegal drugs are more dangerous and more expensive. The risk of cardiac arrest with cocaine is about twenty-five times as high as in the absence of the drug; the risk of death from an overdose of heroin is even greater. A person who injects, smokes, or sniffs a white powder, without knowing where that powder came from or how it was produced, is engaging in an inherently dangerous activity.

But violence in these circumstances, especially in the inner cities of North America, does not flow so much from the consumption of heroin or cocaine as it does from the manner in which the trade is regulated. The cost of dependence on such drugs can run into hundreds or even thousands of dollars a week, leading addicts to steal, rob, break and enter, and even kill to obtain a fix. Further, when arguments arise among distributors, violence is ultimately the only means of resolving the dispute.

Drug abuse, legal and illegal, is a global problem of substantial proportions. In the United States, Canada, and Western Europe, human beings use too many drugs too often, in ways that are clearly destructive to health, family, and community. But because of a global prohibition, that small part of the citizenry who become dependent on cocaine and heroin (typically less than 1 per cent of any nation's population) have been transformed into criminals, rather than individuals who have profound difficulties with substance abuse. Heroin and cocaine abuse is only the tip of the iceberg; these people usually have even more severe problems with alcohol, tobacco, and prescription drugs.

The difficulties are exacerbated when recreational users and hard-core addicts are sent to prison for their crimes of consumption. Thousands of men, some of them with drug problems, are now living with each other, fostering a kind of synergistic infection, especially for intravenous users. In the sphere of illegal drugs, what was seen at the turn of the century as a matter of private indulgence or weakness has been transformed into a public evil.

Both the consumption of alcohol and the illegal status of drugs such as cannabis, cocaine, and heroin increase the potential for male violence. Alcohol adds an unacceptable level of risk for those who are easily provoked and who view violence as an appropriate social response to interpersonal conflict. And our failure to regulate the trade in illegal drugs—a trade that caters to desperate men in desperate social circumstances, often armed with handguns—markedly increases the potential for male violence. (This is what the high homicide rate in Washington, D.C., is all about.) If we can begin to view alcohol as a drug, and drug abuse as a major public health problem, rather than an issue of morality that needs to be controlled by the justice system, we may be able to substantially stem the tide of male violence that has washed over the Western world in the last thirty or forty years.

Stop Glorifying Male Violence

Television and film glorify men who use violence to solve social problems. But censorship is no solution; it drives the appetite for violence underground, where it is more difficult to monitor and comprehend. In addition, censorship has, historically, always been applied against minorities—homosexuals, trade unionists, innovative artists. Moreover, image and reality are often fairly separated; there is nothing inherently wrong with escapism and fantasy, whether in the realm of sexuality or of violence.

A better strategy is to speak out against male violence in the home, in the community, and in the classroom. Education remains the most legitimate and hopeful strategy for responding to this complex problem. Additionally, we should not give economic support to films that do little else than portray violence as a solution to social problems, and we must stop patronizing professional hockey until the sport takes take steps to eliminate fighting as a part of the game. Why not give basketball, soccer, and baseball a chance? At least these professional leagues won't permit a man who has thrown a punch to remain in the game. And we must recognize that the government, whether at the national, provincial, state, or municipal level, has a responsibility to oppose social institutions that glorify violence.

Support Men Who Are Biologically and Environmentally at Risk
Some men have a greater risk of violent behaviour than others, for both biological and environmental reasons. And our culture has tended to downplay biology, preferring to believe, contrary to evidence, that environment is inevitably more important. We endorse the malleability of human beings—the notion that anyone can succeed if only he or she works hard enough. Persistence, dedication, and diligence are seen as the keys to success. As the Baltimore-based conglomerate of Sylvan Learning Centers says in its television ads, "Success Is Learned."

But the characteristics of a young male who is at the greatest risk of committing a criminal offence are both inherent in the individual and created by the environment in which he lives. An extensive criminological literature points to this combination of risk factors: being male, having low socioeconomic status, having little family cohesiveness, being suspended or expelled from school, having learning disabilities, making unproductive use of leisure time, having criminal associations, having a poor employment history, having unpleasant and difficult personality characteristics (an inability to form meaningful attachments, hyperactivity, bizarre thought and affect, and withdrawal from contact with others). Several of these characteristics have a biological origin: being male, having problems at school, having a poor employment history, and having problems related to certain personality characteristics.

There is widespread social acceptance of the idea that talented parents, whether in the realm of athletics or educational achievement, are likely to have offspring with similar kinds of talents. But the less easily accepted corollary of this finding is that children of parents who have learning difficulties and problem personalities are equally likely to have difficulties—with school, with employment, and in forming meaningful relationships.

Environment often exacerbates the problems of those with compromised abilities and difficult personalities. Abuse and neglect create further liabilities, as do having a family that is unable to care or cope and spending time with other young men who are involved in criminal activity.

During the past fifteen years I have spoken with many murderers and other men convicted of violent offences; I have watched them as they have left jail, in some cases never to return, in others to return within a matter of months. Those who succeed are those who are most realistic about who they are, about their strengths and limitations, and about their vulnerabilities. Those who avoid more conflict have recognized that they must not put themselves into situations where they might revert to old ways.

On a more practical level, they change some of their behaviour. For example, they don't frequent down-and-out bars or become involved in the trade in illegal drugs; both are recipes for conflict and violence. One murderer, out of jail for almost two decades, told me that he knows he has a short fuse. "I have demons that other people don't have; I stay away from alcohol and drugs, and I'm very slow to become involved with other people. I have to develop a lot of trust before I feel at all comfortable."

For the last thirty years, Newfoundland has had one of the lowest rates of homicide in the world. British Columbia has about five times as many killings, despite identical legislation for homicide and identical punishment. This fact in itself must cast doubt on the notion that punishment is the most important deterrent to violent crime. Washington, D.C., where the death penalty is in effect, has more than fifty times as many killings as Newfoundland.

When I asked the chief homicide detective of the Royal Newfoundland Constabulary why Newfoundland has such a low rate of homicide, he responded that Newfoundlanders are contented with their lot in life and that Newfoundland is made up of small communities, in St. John's, in the outports, in the little fishing villages that dot the coastline. "Can you imagine," he asked, "the shame that would fall on you and your family and your victim's family if such a thing should happen?"

In other words, the lives of the people of Newfoundland are intertwined in a way that is totally different from the transience of so many of North America's urban landscapes. The family is part of a larger community, and in the context of these shared lives, homicide becomes unthinkable.

Let me give you one other example of the importance of family and community. In 1987 Robbie Robidoux was released from a Canadian penitentiary, after spending seventeen of his thirty-five years in either juvenile detention or adult institutions. He had a long record of violent offences, stretching from his teenage years to his thirties; he was declared a dangerous offender in 1984. But in the mid-1980s he became determined to change his life. He enrolled in university programs, started training to run a marathon, and stayed away from the prison trade in illegal drugs.

One of my colleagues at the university was instrumental in helping Robbie leave his violent past behind. Curt would escort Robbie from the jail to his class on campus and back, spending several hours every week driving him to and from the start of a new life. When Robbie did gain his release, he came to live on campus, far from the bars of Vancouver's downtown east side. He was never a very good student, but he was determined to meet his goal of helping kids at risk.

He established a network of people in the community who cared about his welfare—prison activists, educators, lawyers, and other students—and he made sure that he kept in touch with all of them. It certainly wasn't all smooth sailing, but eventually he was able to find employment as a street worker, a job that he has kept for the past seven years. He now has a live-in relationship, a cat named Brew, and a vegetable garden. His long-term goal is the metaphorical house with a white picket fence.

How has he accomplished this change of life? First, with his own strong will to succeed, and second, with the support of his live-in companion, his network of friends, and a community that is willing to accept a man who can turn his life around.

Support Children Who Are Biologically and Environmentally at Risk

But it is not what we do to such young men as adults that is most critical. It is the way in which children at risk are treated in those crucial first years of life that will make all the difference. If we are sincere about ridding ourselves of male violence, we must also take steps to ensure that such children are well cared for: communities and governments must take more responsibility, not less—for day-care centres and for recreational, vocational, and academic opportunities. This need not involve an elaborate government bureaucracy but rather a community commitment to a better life for children at risk.

It can only be determined through trial and error what specific programs and what kinds of assistance are most likely to help. If we want a kinder and gentler society, that critical investment of time, energy, and capital must be found. There is a better way for men and for women; male biology has been our handicap and will likely continue to be, but it is not our destiny.

Robbie Robidoux and many others might have been able to avoid many years in federal prisons if we, as a society, had given more than lip service to the need to build strong families and communities. Most boys are socialized by their parents and communities to respect the rights and property of others, but in some families this just doesn't happen. The parents may be alcoholic and abusive or may have limited abilities and limited horizons. In North America today people who have such difficulties are reproducing more quickly than people who don't have such difficulties. Sadly, these folks often don't know or don't care about birth control; they usually believe, despite all evidence to the contrary, that having a child will bring order to a chaotic and desperately unhappy life.

Our society needs to be more involved with these at-risk children and to provide more focused care. In the ghettos of North

America, where crime and violence are at their peak, we need free, licensed daycare centres, staffed by caring and competent individuals who can identify problems and begin to address them. There's no use in objecting that the family should be responsible in such circumstances. Of course it should, but these are folks who are simply not willing or able to cope—they need assistance.

Recognize and Harness the Strengths of the Male

Although the superior size, strength, and speed of the male provide a physical advantage in most conflicts with women, and although every male is also anatomically constructed to be a potential rapist, there are other, more positive aspects of being male that should not be ignored or overlooked. Male size, strength, speed, and superior spatial ability convey collective benefits in every culture.

Since 1904 the Carnegie Hero Fund Commission has given awards to individuals in the United States or Canada who risk or sacrifice their lives "in saving or attempting to save the life of a fellow human being." In the ninety years in which the Hero Fund Commission has been in place, more than seven thousand medals have been awarded; in more than 90 per cent of these cases the recipient has been male.

Helping a stranger in difficulty is a critical form of altruism, closely linked to the biological strengths of the male. When psychologists have studied altruistic behaviour in experimental settings, they have found that men are more helpful. Specifically, men are more likely than women to help a person with car trouble on a busy street, to report a theft by a shoplifter, to lend a dime to a woman in a park, to help a man who has fallen in the subway, or to donate money to the March of Dimes. In these short-term encounters with strangers, knowledge of male biology would predict that men will provide more help than women, and that women will receive more help than men—and this is what happens. There is one caveat, however, before there is a rush to announce that males are the more altruistic and giving of the sexes. Researchers have noted that male abilities falter when altruism isn't in the context of risk, excitement, or impulsiveness but involves the giving of assistance to intimates within long-term relationships. In this context, women appear to be more helpful.

There is much to celebrate in the human male. There is something to be said for "the strong, silent type," working diligently and taking risks to support his family. We must resist a political correctness that argues that this stereotype is entirely a product of our culture. And we must not continue to indulge ourselves in the fanciful belief that male behaviour is entirely or even predominantly socially determined. If we are to harness the strengths of the male without perpetuating the bloody trail of corpses that has been our legacy, we can no longer pretend that we are all blank slates, waiting for the hand of culture to descend upon us.

Notes

Chapter One: The Trouble with Men

Page 2: "I'll wait forever . . . ," "Holtam insists he's innocent as he gets 25 years in prison," *Vancouver Sun*, December 3, 1999, p. 1.

Page 3: "This is the honest . . . ," ibid., p. 2.

Page 3: "Men often hunt down . . . ," Margo Wilson and Martin Daly, "Who Kills Whom in Spouse Killings? On the Exceptional Sex Ratio of Spousal Homicides in the United States," *Criminology* 30, no. 2 (1992): 206.

Page 5: "His long history of abnormal behavior . . . ," letter from Dr. E. B. Cahoon to Hugh Latimer, June 1, 1961, p. 2, Owen "Mickey" Feener, Capital Case Files, RG 13 Series, National Archives of Canada, Ottawa.

Page 5: "his extremely poor judgement . . . ," letter from Dr. R. Keeler to Hugh Latimer, June 1, 1961, p. 2, Owen "Mickey" Feener, Capital Case Files, RG 13 Series, National Archives of Canada, Ottawa.

Page 6: "rather sly" and "ill-uses his younger brother . . . ," report from Department of Public Welfare, May 26, 1961, p. 1, Owen "Mickey" Feener, Capital Case Files, RG 13 Series, National Archives of Canada, Ottawa.

Page 6: "While he was here . . . ," quoted in Royal Canadian Mounted Police Report, April 24, 1961, p. 1, Owen "Mickey" Feener, Capital Case Files, RG 13 Series, National Archives of Canada, Ottawa.

Page 6: "I have known him . . . ," letter to the Solicitor-General from Mrs. Roy Feener, May 25, 1961, p. 1, Owen "Mickey" Feener, Capital Case Files, RG 13 Series, National Archives of Canada, Ottawa.

Page 16: "our social natures are . . . ," Martin Daly and Margo Wilson, *Homicide* (New York: Aldine de Gruyter, 1988), 153.

Page 17: "To be vulnerable is to be invincible . . . ," Robert Hughes, *Culture of Complaint: A Passionate Look into the Ailing Heart of America* (New York: Warner, 1994).

Page 20: "neither biology or psychology . . . ," Marvin Wolfgang, "Family Violence and Criminal Behavior," in *Violence and Responsibility,* ed. R. L. Sadoff, (New York: Spectrum, 1978), 87.

Page 20: "Knowing only the facts . . . ," Marvin Harris, *Cows, Pigs, Wars and Witches* (New York: Random House, 1972), 84.

Chapter Two: The Evolution of Male Violence

Page 30: "arcadian existence of primal innocence," Robert Ardrey, *The Territorial Imperative* (London: Atheneum, 1996), 222.

Pages 30–31: "One year later . . . ," Richard Wrangham and Dale Peterson, *Demonic Males: Apes and the Origins of Human Violence* (New York: Houghton Mifflin, 1996), 16–17.

Page 33: "One by one . . . ," ibid., 17.

Pages 39–40: "A big smile . . . ," Roger Fouts, *Next of Kin: My Conversations with Chimpanzees* (New York: Avon Books, 1997), 355–56.

Page 46: "we found a genuine . . . ," Margaret Mead, *Sex and Temperament in Three Primitive Societies* (New York: William Morrow, 1935).

Page 51: "A polygynous nation . . . ," Robert Wright, *The Moral Animal / Why We Are the Way We Are: The New Science of Evolutionary Psychology* (New York: Pantheon, 1994), 101.

Page 54: "The founding myth . . . ," Matt Ridley, *The Red Queen: Sex and the Evolution of Human Nature* (London: Penguin, 1993), 197–98.

Pages 56–57: "The original meaning . . . ," Jonathan Weiner, *The Beak of the Finch: A Story of Evolution in Our Time* (New York: Vintage Books, 1995), 299–300.

Chapter Three: Sex Differences and the Dark Heart of Political Correctness

Page 67: "This has become . . . ," Patricia Pearson, *When She Was Bad: Violent Women and the Myth of Innocence* (Toronto: Random House, 1997), 32.

Pages 67–68: "I had this thing . . . ," interview with Dirk Rochester, convicted murderer, in penitentiary, 1987. Dirk Rochester and Sally Brennan are both pseudonyms.

Page 68: "We continued quarrelling . . . ," police report, Peter Beyak, Capital Case Files, 1937, RG 13 Series, National Archives of Canada, Ottawa.

Page 74: "women feel socially empowered . . ." and "matrilineal kinship networks . . . ," Margo Wilson and Martin Daly, "Who Kills Whom in Spouse Killings? On the Exceptional Sex Ratio of Spousal Homicides in the United States," *Criminology* 30, no. 2 (1992): 208.

Page 76: "We favor the hypothesis . . . ," Camilla Benbow and Julian Stanley, "Sex Differences in Mathematical Ability: Fact or Artifact?" *Science* 210 (1980): 1264.

Page 76: "environmental and cultural factors . . . ," Alice Schafer and Mary Gray, "Sex and Mathematics," *Science* 211 (1981): 231.

Page 77: "If your mother hates math . . . ," Sheila Tobias, quoted in "Do Males Have a Math Gene?" *Newsweek,* December 15, 1980, p. 73.

Page 77: "what we have here . . . ," Elaine Newman, biology professor at Concordia University, quoted in "Boys Beat Girls in Controversial Study," *Globe and Mail,* September 3, 1981, Toronto edition.

Page 77: "the only permissible . . . ," Benbow and Stanley, 1264.

Page 81: "do not define anything . . . ," Stephen Jay Gould, *The Mismeasure of Man* (New York: W. W. Norton, 1981), 155.

Page 84: "There are no gender differences . . . ," Janet Shibley Hyde and Marcia Linn, "Gender Differences in Verbal Ability: A Meta-Analysis," *Psychological Bulletin* 104, no. 1 (1988): 62.

Page 86: "nothing more than . . . ," Susan Brownmiller, *Against Our Will: Men, Women and Rape* (New York: Bantam Books, 1976), 5.

Pages 88–89: Statistics are from Robert T. Michael, et al., *Sex in America: A Definitive Survey* (London: Little, Brown, 1994).

Page 91: "A pinup at work . . . ," Warren Farrell, *The Myth of Male Power* (New York: Berkley Books, 1996), 302–3.

Page 93: "Two lessons emerge . . . ," Robert Pool, *Eve's Rib: Searching for the Biological Roots of Sex Differences* (New York: Crown, 1994), 255.

Chapter Four: Bred in the Bone

Page 96: "Was there some need . . . ," Jonathan Kellerman, *Savage Spawn: Reflections on Violent Children* (New York: Ballantine, 1999), 104.

Page 98: All quotes are on this page are from Cesare Lombroso, quoted in Gina Lombroso-Ferrero, *Criminal Man: According to the Classification of Cesare Lombroso* (Montclair, N.J.: Patterson Smith, 1972).

Page 105: "a relatively good . . . ," Michael Bohman, "Predisposition to Criminality: Swedish Adoption Studies in Retrospect," in *Genetics of Criminal and Antisocial Behavior,* ed. Gregory R. Bock and Jamie A. Goode (Chichester: John Wiley and Sons, 1995), 100.

Page 109: All quotes on this page are from the California Psychological Inventory.

Chapter Five: The Testosterone Connection

Pages 116–17: "The object of . . . ," Dr. Edward Berdoe, letter to British physicians, July 1889.

Page 121: "Obviously, if you over-treat . . . ," quoted in the *Vancouver Sun,* August 1998.

Page 134: "there is some indirect . . . ," John Archer, "The Influence of Testosterone on Human Aggression," *British Journal of Psychology* 82 (1991): 21.

Chapter Six: Environment Matters

Page 142: Statistics are from Paul and Patricia Brantingham, *Patterns in Crime* (New York: Macmillan, 1984), chapters 7 and 8, 119–210.

Page 143: Ibid.

Page 144: Statistics are from John Conway, *The Canadian Family in Crisis* (James Lorimer, 1990), 11–36.

Page 146: "I hope you're happy now . . ." and "just flipped right out," interview with Kevin Bourne, convicted murderer, in penitentiary, 1987. Kevin Bourne is a pseudonym.

Page 147: "Did you have a good lay?" Interview with Ben Costello, convicted murderer, in penitentiary, 1987. Ben Costello is a pseudonym.

Page 147: "If you love . . ." and "I'll give you a . . . ," interview with Victor Morrison, convicted murderer, in penitentiary, 1987. Victor Morrison is a pseudonym.

Page 148: "but a minute's worth . . . ," Warren Farrell, *The Myth of Male Power* (New York: Berkley Books, 1996), 220.

Page 148: "missing contact with men" and "what is missing . . . ," Robert Bly, quoted in Susan Faludi, *Backlash: The Undeclared War against American Women* (New York: Crown, 1991), 306.

Page 149: "Men young and old . . . ," Steve Chapple and David Talbot, quoted in ibid., 310.

Page 150: "an undeclared war . . . ," ibid., chapter 1, 281–331.

Page 159: "I'm going to tell . . . ," interview with Scott Millar, convicted murderer, in penitentiary, 1987. Scott Millar is a pseudonym.

Page 162: Statistics are from Canadian Centre for Justice Statistics, Statistics Canada, Ottawa. See for specific detail *The Juristat Reader* (Toronto: Thompson Publishing, 1999).

Page 165: "Well, there was physical abuse . . . ," interview with Tom Pickard, convicted murderer, in penitentiary, 1987. Tom Pickard is a pseudonym.

Page 165: "an alcoholic of the worst type . . . ," statement of Jack Roberts, p. 1, Louis Fisher, Capital Case Files, 1960, RG 13 Series, National Archives of Canada, Ottawa.

Page 166: "very unhappy," interview with Leonard Peete, convicted murderer, in penitentiary, 1987. Leonard Peete is a pseudonym.

Chapter Seven: Calming the Beast

Page 172: "One reason children differ . . . ," James Q. Wilson, review of *Why They Kill: The Discoveries of a Maverick Criminologist,* by Richard Rhodes, *Manchester Guardian,* November 1999.

Pages 174–75: "The women were all . . . ," Robert Pool, *Eve's Rib: Searching for the Biological Roots of Sex Differences* (New York: Crown, 1994), 52.

Pages 183–84: "I have demons . . . ," conversation with convicted murderer, 1998.

Page 184: "Can you imagine . . . ," interview with Detective Len Power, Royal Newfoundland Constabulary, St. John's, Newfoundland, June 1989.

Further Reading

Chapter Two: The Evolution of Male Violence

Daly, Martin, and Margo Wilson. *Homicide*. New York: Aldine de Gruyter, 1988.
A very interesting, thoughtful, and challenging interpretation of homicide, from the perspective of evolutionary psychology.

Diamond, Jared. *The Third Chimpanzee: The Evolution and Future of the Human Animal*. New York: Harper Collins, 1992.
Diamond, Jared. *Guns, Germs and Steel: The Fates of Human Societies*. New York: W. W. Norton, 1999.
Two exceptional books, cataloguing a remarkable sweep of human history and having much to say, historically, about male violence and genocide.

Fouts, Roger. *Next of Kin: My Conversations with Chimpanzees*. New York: Avon Books, 1997.
A wonderfully moving, thoughtful, and at times amusing chronicle of the author's life with chimpanzees.

Leakey, Richard, and Roger Lewin. *Origins Reconsidered: In Search of What Makes Us Human*. New York: Doubleday, 1992.
A very accessible accounting of the process of evolution.

Weiner, Jonathan. *The Beak of the Finch: A Story of Evolution in Our Time*. New York: Vintage Books, 1995.
An evocative and eloquent description of the relatively constant process of evolution, focusing on the Galápagos and the fate of Darwin's finches.

Wrangham, Richard, and Dale Peterson. *Demonic Males: Apes and the Origins of Human Violence*. New York: Houghton Mifflin, 1996.
A controversial and intriguing interpretation of the origins of human violence, pointing to the bonobos as an alternative to our current legacy.

Chapter Three: Sex Differences and the Dark Heart of Political Correctness

Blum, Deborah. *Sex on the Brain: The Biological Differences between Men and Women*. New York: Viking, 1997.
Moir, Anne, and David Jessel. *Brain Sex: The Real Difference between Men and Women*. London: Mandarin, 1991.
Two books that speak to the biology of sex differences, although not with the careful clarity and caveats of Robert Pool's text.

Pool, Robert. *Eve's Rib: Searching for the Biological Roots of Sex Differences*. New York: Crown, 1994.
A well-written, thoughtful, and very comprehensive survey of sex differences, from an author committed to the moral and political equality of men and women.

Academic journals are also a particularly useful source of information about sex differences in abilities, temperament, and aggression. Some key articles follow:

Benbow, Camilla Persson. "Sex Differences in Mathematical Reasoning Ability in Intellectually Talented Preadolescents: Their Nature, Effects, and Possible Causes." *Behavioral and Brain Sciences* 11 (1988): 169–232.

Eagly, Alice, and Maureen Crowley. "Gender and Helping Behavior: A Meta-Analytic Review of the Social Psychological Literature." *Psychological Bulletin* 100, no. 3 (1986): 283–308.

Eaton, Warren, and Lesley Reid Enns. "Sex Differences in Human Motor Activity Level." *Psychological Bulletin* 100, no. 1 (1986): 19–28.

Hoffman, Martin. "Sex Differences in Empathy and Related Behaviors." *Psychological Bulletin* 84, no. 4 (1977): 712–22.

Hyde, Janet Shibley, and Marcia Linn. "Gender Differences in Verbal Ability: A Meta-Analysis." *Psychological Bulletin* 104, no. 1 (1988): 53–69.

Strube, Michael J. "Meta-Analysis and Cross-Cultural Comparison: Sex Differences in Child Competitiveness." *Journal of Cross-Cultural Psychology* 12, no. 1 (1981): 3–20.

Thomas, Jerry, and Karen French. "Gender Differences across Age in Motor Performance: A Meta-Analysis." *Psychological Bulletin* 98, no. 2 (1985): 260–82.

Voyer, Daniel; Susan Voyer; and M. P. Bryden. "Magnitude of Sex Differences in Spatial Abilities: A Meta-Analysis and Consideration of Critical Variables." *Psychological Bulletin* 117, no. 2 (1995): 250–70.

Chapter Four: Bred in the Bone

Kellerman, Jonathan. *Savage Spawn: Reflections on Violent Children.* New York: Ballantine, 1999.
A passionate critique of our society's failure to recognize the difficulties posed by the criminality and behaviour of a small number of very disturbed children.

Lombroso-Ferrero, Gina. *Criminal Man: According to the Classification of Cesare Lombroso.* Montclair, N.J.: Patterson Smith, 1972.
Sheldon, W. H., with the collaboration of S. S. Stevens and W. B. Tucker. *The Varieties of Human Physique.* New York: Harper, 1940.
Sheldon, W. H., with the collaboration of E. M. Hartl and E. McDermott. *Varieties of Delinquent Youth.* New York: Harper, 1949.
A few of the early attempts (often entertaining) to understand why some men are more violent than others, using a relatively unsophisticated understanding of biology as a base for comprehension.

Mednick, S. A.; W. F. Gabrielli Jr.; and B. Hutchings. "Genetic Influences in Criminal Convictions: Evidence from an Adoption Cohort." *Science* 224 (1984): 891–94.
Mednick, S. A.; "Genetic Factors in the Etiology of Criminal Behavior." In *The Causes of Crime: New Biological Approaches,* edited by S. A. Mednick,

Terri E. Moffit, and Susan A. Stock. Cambridge: Cambridge University
Press, 1987.
*In cumulative terms, a compelling presentation of evidence that makes clear
that some children are more likely to engage in crime than others, for reasons
that can be traced to their genes.*

Chapter Five: The Testosterone Connection

Albert, D. J.; M. L. Walsh; and R. H. Jonik. "Aggression in Humans: What Is
Its Biological Foundation?" *Neuroscience and Biobehavioral Reviews* 17
(1993): 405–25.
*A thorough review article arguing against a connection between testosterone
and aggression.*

Archer, John. "The Influence of Testosterone on Human Aggression." *British
Journal of Psychology* 82 (1991): 1–28.
*A thorough review article suggesting that there is an important relationship
between testosterone and aggression, albeit one that is far from causal.*

Wille, Reinhard, and Klaus Beier. "Castration in Germany." *Annals of Sex
Research* 2 (1989): 103–33.
*A review article documenting the consequences of castration on subsequent
criminal behaviour.*

Chapter Six: Environment Matters

Archer, Dane, and Rosemary Gartner. *Violence and Crime in Cross-National
Perspective.* New Haven: Yale University Press, 1984.
*This book provides a useful overview of violence and crime in an
international context.*

Brantingham, Paul and Patricia. *Patterns in Crime.* New York: Macmillan,
1984.
*This book compares crime in Canada, the United States, and Britain from
medieval England to the present. An excellent source of information about
temporal and spatial variations in crime.*

Boyd, Neil. *The Last Dance: Murder in Canada*. Scarborough, Ont.: Prentice-Hall, 1988.

Silverman, Robert, and Leslie Kennedy. *Deadly Deeds: Murder in Canada*. Scarborough, Ont.: Nelson, 1993.

Wolfgang, Marvin, *Patterns in Criminal Homicide*. Philadelphia: University of Pennsylvania Press, 1958.
These three books deal with the specifics of homicide in Canada and the United States. See also in this context:

Gartner, Rosemary, "The Victims of Homicide: A Temporal and Cross-National Comparison." *American Sociological Review* 55, no. 1 (1990): 92–106.

Hagan, John. "Comparing Crime and Criminalization in Canada and the U.S.A." *Canadian Journal of Sociology* 14, no. 3 (1989): 361–71.

Friedman, Lawrence. *Crime and Punishment in American History*. New York: Basic Books, 1993.
An interesting history of the U.S. approach to the problems of crime and punishment.

References

Adler, F. *Sisters in Crime.* New York: McGraw-Hill, 1975.

Albert, D.J.; M.L. Walsh; and R.H. Jonik. "Aggression in Humans: What Is Its Biological Foundation?" *Neuroscience and Biobehavioral Reviews* 17 (1993): 405–25.

Alington, Diane, and Russell Leaf. "Elimination of SAT-Verbal Sex Differences Was Due to Policy-Guided Changes in Item Content." *Psychological Reports* 68 (1991): 541–42.

Anderson, R.A.; J. Bancroft; and F.C. Wu. "The Effects of Exogenous Testosterone on Sexuality and Mood of Normal Men." *Journal of Clinical Endocrinology and Metabolism* 75 (1992): 1503–7.

Archer, Dane, and Rosemary Gartner. *Violence and Crime in Cross-National Perspective.* New Haven: Yale University Press, 1984.

Archer, John. "The Influence of Testosterone on Human Aggression." *British Journal of Psychology* 82 (1991): 1–28.

Archer, John. ed. *Male Violence.* London: Routledge, 1994.

Baker, Mary Anne, ed. *Sex Differences in Human Performance.* New York: John Wiley and Sons, 1987.

Beattie, J.M. "Violence and Society in Early-Modern England." In *Perspectives in Criminal Law: Essays in Honour of John Ll. J. Edwards,* edited by A.N. Doob and Edward L. Greenspan. Aurora, Ont.: Canada Law Book, 1985.

Benbow, Camilla Persson. "Sex Differences in Mathematical Reasoning Ability in Intellectually Talented Preadolescents: Their Nature, Effects, and Possible Causes." *Behavioral and Brain Sciences* 11 (1988): 169–232.

Benbow, Camilla Persson, and Julian Stanley. "Sex Differences in Mathematical Ability: Fact or Artifact?" *Science* 210 (1980): 1262–64.

Berenbaum, Sheri, and Melissa Hines. "Early Androgens Are Related to Childhood Sex-Typed Toy Preferences." *Psychological Science* 3, no. 3 (1992): 203–6.

Bohman, Michael. "Predisposition to Criminality: Swedish Adoption Studies in Retrospect." In *Genetics of Criminal and Antisocial Behaviour,* edited by Gregory R. Bock and Jamie A. Goode. Chichester: John Wiley and Sons, 1995.

Bohman, M.; C. R. Cloniger; S. Sigvardson; and A. L. von Knorrin. "Predisposition to Petty Criminality in Swedish Adoptees. 1. Genetic and Environmental Heterogeneity." *Archives of General Psychiatry* 39 (1982): 1233–41.

Boyd, Neil. *The Last Dance: Murder in Canada.* Scarborough, Ont.: Prentice-Hall, 1988.

Brantingham, Paul and Patricia. *Patterns in Crime.* New York: Macmillan, 1984.

Brennan, Patricia; Sarnoff Mednick; and Bjorn Jacobsen. "Assessing the Role of Genetics in Crime Using Adoption Cohorts." In *Genetics of Criminal and Antisocial Behaviour,* edited by Gregory R. Bock and Jamie A. Goode. Chichester: John Wiley and Sons, 1995.

Brownmiller, Susan. *Against Our Will: Men, Women and Rape.* New York: Bantam Books, 1976.

Buss, David. *The Evolution of Desire.* New York: Basic Books, 1994.

Campbell, Anne. *Men, Women and Aggression.* New York: Basic Books, 1993.

Choi, P. Y.; A. C. Parrott; and D. Cowan. "High-Dose Anabolic Steroids in Strength Athletes: Effects upon Hostility and Aggression." *Human Psychopharmacology* 5 (1990): 349–56.

Christen, Yves. *Sex Differences: Modern Biology and the Unisex Fallacy.* London: Transaction, 1991.

Christiansen, Kerrin, and Rainer Knussmann. "Androgen Levels and Components of Aggressive Behavior in Men." *Hormones and Behavior* 21 (1987): 170–80.

Christiansen, Kerrin, and Eike-Meinrad Winkler. "Hormonal, Anthropometrical, and Behavioral Correlates of Physical Aggression in !Kung San Men of Namibia." *Aggressive Behavior* 18 (1992): 271–80.

Coburn, Gord. Master's thesis, Simon Fraser University, 1989.

Collaer, Marcia, and Melissa Hines. "Human Behavioral Sex Differences:
A Role for Gonadal Hormones during Early Development?" *Psychological Bulletin* 118, no. 1 (1995): 55–107.

Daly, Martin, and Margo Wilson. "Evolutionary Social Psychology and Family Homicide," *Science* 242 (1988): 519–24.

Daly, Martin, and Margo Wilson. *Homicide.* New York: Aldine de Gruyter, 1988.

Denno, Deborah. "Legal Implications of Genetics and Crime Research."
In *Genetics of Criminal and Antisocial Behaviour,* edited by Gregory R. Bock and Jamie A. Goode. Chichester: John Wiley and Sons, 1995.

Diamond, Jared. *The Third Chimpanzee: The Evolution and Future of the Human Animal.* New York: HarperCollins, 1992.

Dineen, Tana. *Manufacturing Victims: What the Psychology Industry Is Doing to People.* Toronto: Robert Davies, 1996.

Eagly, Alice, and Maureen Crowley. "Gender and Helping Behavior: A Meta-Analytic Review of the Social Psychological Literature." *Psychological Bulletin* 100, no. 3 (1986): 283–308.

Eagly, Alice, and Valerie Steffen. "Gender and Aggressive Behavior: A Meta-Analytic Review of the Social Psychological Literature." *Psychological Bulletin* 100, no. 3 (1986): 309–30.

Eaton, Warren, and Lesley Reid Enns. "Sex Differences in Human Motor Activity Level." *Psychological Bulletin* 100, no. 1 (1986): 19–28.

Eisler, Riane. *The Chalice and the Blade: Our History, Our Future.* San Francisco: Harper San Francisco, 1988.

Elias, Michael. "Serum Cortisol, Testosterone, and Testosterone-Binding Globulin Responses to Competitive Fighting in Human Males." *Aggressive Behavior* 7 (1981): 215–24.

Eveleth, Phyllis, and James Tanner. *Worldwide Variation in Human Growth.* 2d ed. Cambridge: Cambridge University Press, 1990.

Eysenck, H. J. *Crime and Personality.* London: Routledge and Kegan Paul, 1977.

Faludi, Susan. *Backlash: The Undeclared War against American Women.* New York: Crown, 1991.

Farrell, Warren. *The Myth of Male Power.* New York: Berkley Books, 1996.

Fausto-Sterling, Anne. *Myths of Gender.* Rev. ed. New York: Basic Books, 1985.

Feld, L.H., and M. Williams. "The Hormonal Treatment of Sexual Offenders." *Medical Science and Law* 10 (1970): 27–34.

Fornes, Paul; Laurent Druilhe; and Dominique Lecomte. "Homicide among Youth and Young Adults, 15 through 29 Years of Age. A Report of 138 Cases from Paris and Its Suburbs, 1991–1993." *Journal of Forensic Sciences* 41, no. 5 (1996): 837–40.

Fouts, Roger. *Next of Kin: My Conversations with Chimpanzees.* New York: Avon Books, 1997.

Freedman, Daniel, and Marilyn DeBoer. "Biological and Cultural Differences in Early Child Development." *Annual Review of Anthropology* 8 (1979): 579–600.

Friedman, Lawrence. *Crime and Punishment in American History.* New York: Basic Books, 1993.

Gibson, Evelyn. *Homicide in England and Wales, 1967–1971: Home Office Research Study No. 31.* London: Her Majesty's Stationery Office, 1975.

Gladue, Brian. "Aggressive Behavioral Characteristics, Hormones, and Sexual Orientation in Men and Women." *Aggressive Behavior* 17 (1991): 313–26.

Gladue, Brian; Michael Boechler; and Kevin McCaul. "Hormonal Response to Competition in Human Males." *Aggressive Behavior* 15 (1989): 409–22.

Gladue, Brian, and Michael Bailey. "Spatial Ability, Handedness, and Human Sexual Orientation." *Psychoneuroendocrinology* 20, no. 5 (1995): 487–97.

Goetting, Ann. *Homicide in Families and Other Special Populations.* New York: Springer, 1995.

Goring, Charles. *The English Convict: A Statistical Study.* London: Darling and Son, 1913.

Gottlieb, Peter, and Gorm Gabrielson. "Alcohol-Intoxicated Homicides in Copenhagen, 1959–1983." *International Journal of Law and Psychiatry* 15, no. 1 (1992): 77–87.

Gough, Harrison G. "Cross-Cultural Validation of a Measure of Asocial Behavior." *Psychological Reports* 17 (1965): 379–87.

Gould, Stephen Jay. *The Panda's Thumb.* New York: W.W. Norton, 1980.

Gould, Stephen Jay. *The Mismeasure of Man.* New York: W.W. Norton, 1981.

Harris, Marvin. *Cows, Pigs, Wars and Witches.* New York: Random House, 1992.

Hartl, Emil; Edward Monnelly; and Roland D. Elderkin. *Physique and Delinquent Behavior: A Thirty Year Follow-Up of William H. Sheldon's Varieties of Delinquent Youth.* New York: Academic Press, 1982.

Herman, John. "Rejuvenation: Brown Sequard to Brinkley." *New York State Journal of Medicine* (1982): 1731–39.

Hindelang, M.J. "Variations in Sex-Race-Age-Specific Incidence Rates of Offending." *American Sociological Review* 46 (1981): 461–74.

Hines, Melissa. "Gonadal Hormones and Human Cognitive Development." In *Hormones, Brain and Behaviour in Vertebrates*, edited by Jacques Balthazart. New York: Karger, Basel, 1990.

Hoffman, Martin. "Sex Differences in Empathy and Related Behaviors." *Psychological Bulletin* 84, no.4 (1977): 712–22.

Holmes, Ronald, and Stephen Holmes. *Murder in America.* Thousand Oaks, Ca.: Sage, 1994.

Hook, E.B. "Behavior Implications of the Human xyy Genotype." *Science* 179 (1973): 139–50.

Hooton, E.A. *The American Criminal: An Anthropological Study.* Cambridge: Harvard University Press, 1939.

Horgan, Dianne Marie Daugherty. "Language Development: A Cross-Methodological Study." Ph.D. thesis, University of Michigan, 1975.

Hoyenga, Katherine, and Kermit Hoyenga. *The Question of Sex Differences: Psychological, Cultural and Biological Issues.* Boston: Little Brown, 1979.

Hudson, Liam and Bernadine Jacot. *Intimate Relations: The Natural History of Desire.* New Haven: Yale University Press, 1995.

Hughes, Robert. *Culture of Complaint: A Passionate Look into the Ailing Heart of America.* New York: Warner, 1994

Hyde, Janet Shibley, and Marcia Linn. "Gender Differences in Verbal Ability: A Meta-Analysis." *Psychological Bulletin* 104, no. 1 (1988): 53–69.

Hyde, Janet; Elizabeth Fenema; and Susan Lamam. "Gender Differences in Mathematics Performance: A Meta-Analysis." *Psychological Bulletin* 107 (1990): 139–55.

Imperato-McGinley, J.; R.E. Peterson; T. Gautier; and E. Sturla. "Androgens and the Evolution of Male-Gender Identity among Pseudohermaphrodites with 5-reductase Deficiency." *New England Journal of Medicine* 300 (1979): 1233–37.

Imperato-McGinley, J.; M. Pichardo; T. Gautier; O. Voyer; and M.P. Bryden. "Cognitive Abilities in Androgen-Insensitive Subjects: Comparison with Control Males and Females from the Same Kindred." *Clinical Endocrinology* 34 (1991): 341–47.

Jacobs, P. A.; M. Brunton; M. Melville; R. P. Brittain; and W. F. McClemont. "Aggressive Behaviour, Mental Sub-Normality and the xyy Male." *Nature* 208 (1965): 1351–52.

Kellerman, A. L. "Gun Ownership As a Risk Factor for Homicide in the Home." *New England Journal of Medicine* 327 (1993): 1084–91.

Kellerman, Jonathan. *Savage Spawn: Reflections on Violent Children.* New York: Ballantine, 1999.

Kimura, Doreen. "Are Men's and Women's Brains Really Different?" *Canadian Psychology* 28, no. 2 (1987): 133–47.

Kimura, Doreen. "Sex Differences in the Brain." *Scientific American,* September 1992, 118–25.

Knoth, Russell; Kelly Boyd; and B. Singer. "Empirical Test of Sexual Selection Theory: Predictions of Sex Differences in Onset, Intensity and Time Course of Sexual Arousal." *Journal of Sex Research* 24 (1988): 73–89.

Kreuz, L. E., and R. M. Rose. "Assessment of Aggressive Behavior and Plasma Testosterone in a Young Criminal Population." *Psychomatic Medicine* 34 (1972): 321–32.

Laan, Ellen, and Walter Everaerd. "Women's Sexual and Emotional Responses to Male and Female Produced Erotica." *Archives of Sexual Behavior* 23, no. 2 (1994): 153–69.

Lange, Johannes. *Crime As Destiny.* London: Unwin, 1931.

Leakey, Richard, and Roger Lewin. *Origins Reconsidered: In Search of What Makes Us Human.* New York: Doubleday, 1992.

Lerer, Leonard. "Women, Homicide and Alcohol in Cape Town, South Africa." *Forensic Science International* 55, no. 1 (1992): 93–99.

Lester, David. *Patterns of Suicide and Homicide in America.* New York: Nova Science, 1993.

LeVay, Simon. "A Difference in Hypothalamic Structure between Heterosexual and Homosexual Men." *Science* 253 (1991): 1034–37.

Lever, Janet. "Sex Differences in the Games Children Play." *Social Problems* 23 (1976): 478–87.

Lever, Janet. "Sex Differences in the Complexity of Children's Play and Games." *American Sociological Review* 43 (1978): 471–83.

Lewis, Dorothy. "Biopsychosocial Characteristics of Children Who Later Murder: A Prospective Study." *American Journal of Psychiatry* 142 (1985): 1161–67.

Lewis, Dorothy; Shelley S. Shanok; and Jonathan H. Pincus. "The Neuropsy-chiatric Status of Violent Male Juvenile Delinquents." In *Vulnerabilities to Delinquency*, edited by D. O. Lewis. New York: Spectrum, 1981.

Lewis, Michael. "Infants' Responses to Facial Stimuli during the First Year of Life." *Developmental Psychology* 1, no. 2 (1969): 75–86.

Lindqvist, Per. "Criminal Homicide in Northern Sweden 1970–1981: Alcohol Intoxication, Alcohol Abuse and Mental Disease." *International Journal of Law and Psychiatry* 8, no. 1 (1986): 19–36.

Lombroso-Ferrero, Gina. *Criminal Man: According to the Classification of Cesare Lombroso*. Montclair, N.J.: Patterson Smith, 1972.

Lyons, Michael. "A Twin Study of Self-Reported Criminal Behaviour." In *Genetics of Criminal and Antisocial Behaviour*, edited by Gregory R. Bock and Jamie A. Goode. Chichester: John Wiley and Sons, 1995.

Maccoby, E. E., and C. N. Jacklin. *The Psychology of Sex Differences*. Stanford: Stanford University Press, 1974.

Maccoby, E. E., and C. N. Jacklin. "Sex Differences in Aggression: A Rejoinder and Reprise." *Child Development* 51 (1980): 964–80.

Mann, Virginia; Sumiko Sasanuma; Naoko Sakuma; and Shinoba Masaki. "Sex Differences in Cognitive Abilities: A Cross-Cultural Perspective." *Neuropsychologia* 28 (1990): 1063–77.

Martin, David, and H. D. Hoover. "Sex Differences in Educational Achieve-ment: A Longitudinal Study." *Journal of Early Adolescence* 7 (1987): 65–83.

Mazur, Allen, and Theodore Lamb. "Testosterone, Status and Mood in Human Males." *Hormones and Behavior* 14 (1980): 236–46.

McGuiness. "Behavioral Tempo in Pre-School Boys and Girls." *Learning and Individual Differences* 2, no. 3 (1990): 315–25.

Mednick, S. A.; W. F. Gabrielli Jr.; and B. Hutchings. "Genetic Influences in Criminal Convictions: Evidence from an Adoption Cohort." *Science* 224 (1984): 891–94.

Mercier, Charles. *Crime and Criminals: Being the Jurisprudence of Crime, Medical, Biological and Psychological*. London: University of London Press, 1918.

Michael, Robert T; John H. Gagnon; Edward O. Laumann; and Gina Kolata. *Sex in America: A Definitive Survey*. London: Little, Brown, 1994.

Moir, Anne, and David Jessel. *Brain Sex: The Real Difference between Men and Women*. London: Mandarin, 1991.

Money, John. *Love and Love Sickness: The Science of Sex, Gender Difference, and Pair-Bonding.* Baltimore: Johns Hopkins University Press, 1980.

Newburn, Tim, and Elizabeth Stanko. *Just Boys Doing Business? Men, Masculinities and Crime.* London: Routledge, 1994.

Nicholson, John. *Men and Women: How Different Are They?* Oxford: Oxford University Press, 1993.

Notman, Malkah, and Carol Nadelson. *Women and Men: New Perspectives on Gender Differences.* Washington: American Psychiatric Press, 1991.

Overfield, Theresa. *Biologic Variation in Health and Illness: Race, Age and Sex Differences.* 2d ed. New York: CRC Press, 1995.

Pearson, Patricia. *When She Was Bad: Violent Women and the Myth of Innocence.* Toronto: Random House, 1997.

Pool, Robert. *Eve's Rib: Searching for the Biological Roots of Sex Differences.* New York: Crown, 1994.

Rebert, Charles. "Sex Differences in Complex Visuomotor Coordination." *Behavioral and Brain Sciences* 3 (1980): 246–47.

Rhodes, Richard. *Why They Kill: The Discoveries of a Maverick Criminologist.* New York: Knopf, 1999.

Ridley, Matt. *The Red Queen: Sex and the Evolution of Human Nature.* London: Viking, 1993.

Roberts, Julian, and Renate Mohr, eds. *Confronting Sexual Assault: A Decade of Legal and Social Change.* Toronto: University of Toronto Press, 1994.

Roebuck, Julian. *Criminal Typology: The Legalistic, Physical-Constitutional-Hereditary, Psychological-Psychiatric and Sociological Approaches.* Springfield: Ill.: Charles C. Thomas, 1967.

Rossi, Alice. "A Biosocial Perspective on Parenting." *Daedalus* 106, no. 2 (1977): 1–31.

Rossi, Alice. "Gender and Parenthood." In *Gender and the Life Course,* edited by Alice Rossi. New York: Aldine, 1985.

Rubinow, David, and Peter Schmidt. "Androgens, Brain, and Behavior." *American Journal of Psychiatry* 153 (1996): 974–84.

Rubinsky, Hillel, and David Eckerman. "Early-Phase Physiological Response Patterns to Psychosexual Stimuli: Comparison of Male and Female Patterns." *Archives of Sexual Behavior* 16, no. 1 (1987): 45–56.

Rutter, Michael. "Introduction: Concepts of Antisocial Behaviour, of Cause, and of Genetic Influences." In *Genetics of Criminal and Antisocial Behaviour,* edited by Gregory R. Bock and Jamie A. Goode. Chichester: John Wiley and Sons, 1995.

Salvador, Alice; V. Simon; F. Suay; and L. Llorens. "Testosterone and Cortisol Responses to Competitive Fighting in Human Males: A Pilot Study." *Aggressive Behavior* 13 (1987): 9–13.

Schafer, Alice, and Mary Gray. "Sex and Mathematics." *Science* 211 (1981): 231.

Schiebinger, Londa. *Nature's Body: Gender in the Making of Modern Science.* Boston: Beacon Press, 1993.

Sheldon, W. H., with the collaboration of S. S. Stevens and W. B. Tucker. *The Varieties of Human Physique.* New York: Harper, 1940.

Sheldon, W. H., with the collaboration of E. M. Hartl and E. McDermott. *Varieties of Delinquent Youth.* New York: Harper, 1949.

Shields, James, and Eliot Slater. "The Similarity of Diagnostic Problems in Twins and the Biological Specificity in Neuroses and Personality Disturbances." *Evolution Psychiatrique* 31, no. 2 (1966): 441–51.

Silverman, Robert, and Leslie Kennedy. *Deadly Deeds: Murder in Canada.* Scarborough, Ont.: Nelson, 1993.

Simon, Rita, and Jean Landis. *The Crimes That Women Commit, The Punishments They Receive.* Lexington, Mass.: Lexington Books, 1991.

Spunt, Barry; Henry Brownstein; Susan Crimmins; et al. "American Women Who Kill: Self-Reports of Their Homicides." *International Journal of Risk Security and Crime Prevention* 1, no. 4 (1996): 293–303.

Spunt, Barry; Henry Brownstein; Paul Goldstein; Michael Fendrich; et al. "Drug Use by Homicide Offenders." *Journal of Psychoactive Drugs* 27, no. 2 (1995): 125–34.

Statistics Canada. *Homicide in Canada 1976–1985: An Historical Perspective.* Ottawa: Canadian Centre for Justice Statistics, 1987.

Stone, Lawrence. *Uncertain Unions and Broken Lives: Intimate and Revealing Accounts of Marriage and Divorce in England.* Oxford: Oxford University Press, 1992.

Strube, Michael J. "Meta-Analysis and Cross-Cultural Comparison: Sex Differences in Child Competitiveness." *Journal of Cross-Cultural Psychology* 12, no.1 (1981): 3–20.

Su, Tung-Ping; M. Pagliaro; P. S. Schmidt; D. Pickar; J. Wolkowitz; and D. R. Rubinow. "Neuropsychiatric Effects of Anabolic Steroids in Male Normal Volunteers." *Journal of the American Medical Association* 269, no. 21 (1993): 2760–64.

Symposium Report: "Biological Factors in Aggression." *Human Psychopharmacology* 9 (1994): 377–80.

Tannahill, Reay. *Sex in History.* New York: Stein and Day, 1982.

Tannen, Deborah. *You Just Don't Understand: Women and Men in Conversation.* New York: William Morrow, 1990.

Tannen, Deborah. *Gender and Discourse.* New York: Oxford University Press, 1994.

Taylor, Don; Wade C. Meyers; Lynn Robbins; and George W. Barnard. "An Anthropometric Study of Pedophiles and Rapists." *Journal of Forensic Sciences* 38, no. 4 (1993): 765–68.

Thomas, Jerry, and Karen French. "Gender Differences across Age in Motor Performance: A Meta-Analysis." *Psychological Bulletin* 98, no. 2 (1985): 260–82.

Thorne-Finch, Ron. *Ending the Silence: The Origins and Treatment of Male Violence Against Women.* Toronto: University of Toronto Press, 1992.

Tomaselli, Sylvana, and Roy Porter, eds. *Rape.* Oxford: Basil Blackwell, 1986.

Trillin, Calvin. *Killings.* New York: Ticknor and Fields, 1984.

Unnithan, Prabha, et al. *The Currents of Lethal Violence: An Integrated Model of Suicide and Homicide.* Albany: State University of New York Press, 1994.

Van Goozen, Stephanie; Nico Frijda; and Nanne Van de Poll. "Anger and Aggression in Women: Influence of Sports Choice and Testosterone Administration." *Aggressive Behavior* 20 (1994): 213–22.

Voyer, Daniel; Susan Voyer; and M. P. Bryden. "Magnitude of Sex Differences in Spatial Abilities: A Meta-Analysis and Consideration of Critical Variables." *Psychological Bulletin* 117, no. 2 (1995): 250–70.

Weiner, Jonathan. *The Beak of the Finch: A Story of Evolution in Our Time.* New York: Vintage Books, 1995.

Wellings, Kaye; Julia Field; Anne M. Johnson; and Jane Wadsworth. *Sexual Behaviour in Britain: The National Survey of Sexual Attitudes and Lifestyles.* London: Penguin, 1994.

Wille, Reinhard, and Klaus Beier. "Castration in Germany." *Annals of Sex Research* 2 (1989): 103–33.

Willetts, R. F. *Aristocratic Society in Ancient Crete*. London: Routledge and Kegan Paul, 1955.

Wilson, James, and Richard Herrnstein. *Crime and Human Nature: The Definitive Study of the Causes of Crime*. New York: Touchstone, 1985.

Wilson, Margo, and Martin Daly. "Who Kills Whom in Spouse Killings? On the Exceptional Sex Ratio of Spousal Homicides in the United States." *Criminology* 30, no. 2 (1992): 189–215.

Witkin, H. A.; S. A. Mednick; F. Schulsinger; E. Bakkestrom; K. O. Christiansen; D. R. Goodenough; K. Hirschhorn; C. Lundsteen; D. R. Owen; J. Philip; D. B. Rubin; and M. Stocking. "XYY and XXY Men: Criminality and Aggression." *Science* 193 (1976): 547–55.

Wolfgang, Marvin. *Patterns in Criminal Homicide*. Philadelphia: University of Pennsylvania Press, 1958.

Wolfgang, Marvin. "Family Violence and Criminal Behavior." In *Violence and Responsibility*, edited by R. L. Sadoff. New York: Spectrum, 1978.

Wrangham, Richard, and Dale Peterson. *Demonic Males: Apes and the Origins of Human Violence*. New York: Houghton Mifflin, 1996.

Wright, Robert. *The Moral Animal/Why We Are the Way We Are: The New Science of Evolutionary Psychology*. New York: Pantheon, 1994.

Zuckerman, Marvin. *Psychobiology of Personality*. Cambridge: Cambridge University Press, 1991.

Index